Would you like to buy a GOD *in a box?*

How about a mechanical governess guaranteed to be bomb-proof?

Or do you want to see a psi-man about your ailments?

Maybe you'd like to go behind the scenes between today and tomorrow?

Or take the wrong train to the right suburbia?

Any of these things, and many more, make up the astonishing contents of Philip K. Dick's Pandora's Box of science fiction wonders.

Anthony Boucher said of Dick that he combined "a fertile speculative mind" with "the chilling symbolism of absolute nightmare."

SEE FOR YOURSELF.

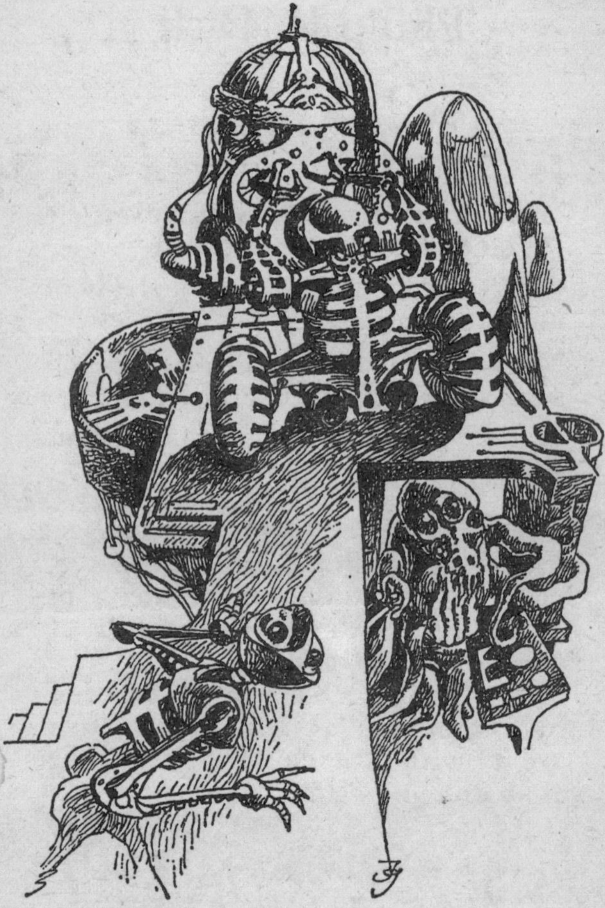

Philip K. Dick

THE BOOK OF PHILIP K. DICK

DAW BOOKS, INC.
DONALD A. WOLLHEIM, PUBLISHER

1301 Avenue of the Americas
New York, N. Y. 10019

COVER BY KAREL THOLE. FRONTISPIECE BY JACK GAUGHAN.

DEDICATION
To Leslie Busby:
The little black-haired girl I love so much

FIRST PRINTING
SECOND PRINTING
THIRD PRINTING
FOURTH PRINTING
FIFTH PRINTING
SIXTH PRINTING
SEVENTH PRINTING
EIGHTH PRINTING
NINTH PRINTING
TENTH PRINTING

FIRST PRINTING, FEBRUARY 1973

DAW BOOKS

PRINTED IN U.S.A.

Table of Contents

NANNY

"WHEN I look back," Mary Fields said, "I marvel that we ever could have grown up without a Nanny to take care of us."

There was no doubt that Nanny had changed the whole life of the Fields's house since she had come. From the time the children opened their eyes in the morning to their last sleepy nod at night, Nanny was in there with them, watching them, hovering about them, seeing that all their wants were taken care of.

Mr. Fields knew, when he went to the office, that his kids were safe, perfectly safe. And Mary was relieved of a countless procession of chores and worries. She did not have to wake the children up, dress them, see that they were washed, ate their meals, or anything else. She did not even have to take them to school. And after school, if they did not come right home, she did not have to pace back and forth in anxiety, worried that something had happened to them.

Not that Nanny spoiled them, of course. When they demanded something absurd or harmful (a whole storeful of candy, or a policeman's motorcycle) Nanny's will was like iron. Like a good shepherd she knew when to refuse the flock its wishes.

Both children loved her. Once, when Nanny had to be sent to the repair shop, they cried and cried without stopping. Neither their mother nor their father could console them. But at last Nanny was back again, and everything was all right. And just in time! Mrs. Fields was exhausted.

"Lord," she said, throwing herself down. "What would we do without her?"

Mr. Fields looked up. "Without who?"

"Without Nanny."

"Heaven only knows," Mr. Fields said.

After Nanny had aroused the children from sleep—by emitting a soft, musical whirr a few feet from their heads—she made certain that they were dressed and down at the breakfast table promptly, with faces clean and dispositions unclouded. If they were cross Nanny allowed them the pleasure of riding downstairs on her back.

Coveted pleasure! Almost like a roller coaster, with Bobby and Jean hanging on for dear life and Nanny flowing down step by step in the funny rolling way she had.

Nanny did not prepare breakfast, of course. That was all done by the kitchen. But she remained to see that the children ate properly and then, when breakfast was over, she supervised their preparations for school. And after they had got their books together and were all brushed and neat, her most important job: seeing that they were safe on the busy streets.

There were many hazards in the city, quite enough to keep Nanny watchful. The swift rocket cruisers that swept along, carrying businessmen to work. The time a bully had tried to hurt Bobby. One quick push from Nanny's starboard grapple and away he went, howling for all he was worth. And the time a drunk started talking to Jean, with heaven knows *what* in mind. Nanny tipped him into the gutter with one nudge of her powerful metal side.

Sometimes the children would linger in front of a store. Nanny would have to prod them gently, urging them on. Or if (as sometimes happened) the children were late to school, Nanny would put them on her back and fairly speed along the sidewalk, her treads buzzing and flapping at a great rate.

After school Nanny was with them constantly, supervising their play, watching over them, protecting them, and at last, when it began to get dark and late, dragging them away from their games and turned in the direction of home.

Sure enough, just as dinner was being set on the table, there was Nanny, herding Bobby and Jean in through the front door, clicking and whirring admonishingly at them.

Just in time for dinner! A quick run to the bathroom to wash their faces and hands.

And at night—

Mrs. Fields was silent, frowning just a little. At night . . . "Tom?" she said.

Her husband looked up from his paper. "What?"

"I've been meaning to talk to you about something. It's very odd, something I don't understand. Of course, I don't know anything about mechanical things. But Tom, at night when we're all asleep and the house is quiet, Nanny—"

There was a sound.

"Mommy!" Jean and Bobby came scampering into the living room, their faces flushed with pleasure. "Mommy, we raced Nanny all the way home, and we won!"

"We won," Bobby said. "We beat her."

"We ran a lot faster than she did," Jean said.

"Where is Nanny, children?" Mrs. Fields asked.

"She's coming. Hello, Daddy."

"Hello, kids," Tom Fields said. He cocked his head to one side, listening. From the front porch came an odd scraping sound, an unusual whirr and scrape. He smiled.

"That's Nanny," Bobby said.

And into the room came Nanny.

Mr. Fields watched her. She had always intrigued him. The only sound in the room was her metal treads, scraping against the hardwood floor, a peculiar rhythmic sound. Nanny came to a halt in front of him, stopping a few feet away. Two unwinking photocell eyes appraised him, eyes on flexible wire stalks. The stalks moved speculatively, weaving slightly. Then they withdrew.

Nanny was built in the shape of a sphere, a large metal sphere, flattened on the bottom. Her surface had been sprayed with a dull green enamel, which had become chipped and gouged through wear. There was not much visible in addition to the eye stalks. The treads could not be seen. On each side of the hull was the outline of a door. From these the magnetic grapples came, when they were needed. The front of the hull came to a point, and there the metal was reinforced. The extra plates welded both fore and aft made her look almost like a weapon of war. A tank of some kind. Or a ship, a rounded metal ship that had come up on land. Or like an insect. A sowbug, as they are called.

"Come on!" Bobby shouted.

Abruptly Nanny moved, spinning slightly as her treads gripped the floor and turned her around. One of her side doors opened. A long metal rod shot out. Playfully, Nanny caught Bobby's arm with her grapple and drew him to her. She perched him on her back. Bobby's legs straddled the metal hull. He kicked with his heels excitedly, jumping up and down.

"Race you around the block!" Jean shouted.

"Giddup!" Bobby cried. Nanny moved away, out of the room with him. A great round bug of whirring metal and relays, clicking photocells and tubes. Jean ran beside her.

There was silence. The parents were alone again.

"Isn't she amazing?" Mrs. Fields said. "Of course, robots are a common sight these days. Certainly more so than a few years ago. You see them everywhere you go, behind counters in stores, driving buses, digging ditches—"

"But Nanny is different," Tom Fields murmured.

"She's—she's not like a machine. She's like a person. A living person. But after all, she's much more complex than any other kind. She has to be. They say she's even more intricate than the kitchen."

"We certainly paid enough for her," Tom said.

"Yes," Mary Fields murmured. "She's very much like a living creature." There was a strange note in her voice. "Very much so."

"She sure takes care of the kids," Tom said, returning to his newspaper.

"But I'm worried." Mary put her coffee cup down, frowning. They were eating dinner. It was late. The two children had been sent up to bed. Mary touched her mouth with her napkin. "Tom, I'm worried. I wish you'd listen to me."

Tom Fields blinked. "Worried? What about?"

"About her. About Nanny."

"Why?"

"I—I don't know."

"You mean we're going to have to repair her again? We just got through fixing her. What is it this time? If those kids didn't get her to—"

"It's not that."

"What, then?"

For a long time his wife did not answer. Abruptly she got up from the table and walked across the room to the stairs. She peered up, staring into the darkness. Tom watched her, puzzled.

"What's the matter?"

"I want to be sure she can't hear us."

"She? Nanny?"

Mary came toward him. "Tom, I woke up last night again. Because of the sounds. I heard them again, the same sounds, the sounds I heard before. And you told me it didn't mean anything!"

Tom gestured. "It doesn't. What does it mean?"

"I don't know. That's what worries me. But after we're all asleep she comes downstairs. She leaves their room. She slips down the stairs as quietly as she can, as soon as she's sure we're all asleep."

"But why?"

"I don't know! Last night I heard her going down, slithering down the stairs, as quiet as a mouse. I heard her moving around down here. And then—"

"Then what?"

"Tom, then I heard her go out the back door. Out, outside the house. She went into the back yard. That was all I heard for awhile."

Tom rubbed his jaw. "Go on."

"I listened. I sat up in bed. You were asleep, of course. Sound asleep. No use trying to wake you. I got up and went to the window. I lifted the shade and looked out. She was out there, out in the back yard."

"What was she doing?"

"I don't know." Mary Fields's face was lined with worry. "I don't know! What in the world *would* a Nanny be doing outside at night, in the back yard?"

It was dark. Terribly dark. But the infrared filter clicked into place, and the darkness vanished. The metal shape moved forward, easing through the kitchen, its treads half-retracted for greatest quiet. It came to the back door and halted, listening.

There was no sound. The house was still. They were all asleep upstairs. Sound asleep.

The Nanny pushed, and the back door opened. It moved out onto the porch, letting the door close gently behind it. The night air was thin and cold. And full of smells, all the strange, tingling smells of the night, when spring has begun to change into summer, when the ground is still moist and the hot July sun has not had a chance to kill all the little growing things.

The Nanny went down the steps, onto the cement path. Then it moved cautiously onto the lawn, the wet blades of grass slapping its sides. After a time it stopped, rising up on its back treads. Its front part jutted up into the air. Its eye stalks stretched, rigid and taut, waving very slightly. Then it settled back down and continued its motion forward.

It was just going around the peach tree, coming back toward the house, when the noise came.

It stopped instantly, alert. Its side doors fell away and its grapples ran out their full lengths, lithe and wary. On the other side of the board fence, beyond the row of shasta daisies, something had stirred. The Nanny peered, clicking filters rapidly. Only a few faint stars winked in the sky overhead. But it saw, and that was enough.

On the other side of the fence a second Nanny was moving, making its way softly through the flowers, coming toward the fence. It was trying to make as little noise as possible. Both Nannies stopped, suddenly unmoving, regarding each other—the green Nanny waiting in its own yard, the blue prowler that had been coming toward the fence.

The blue prowler was a larger Nanny, built to manage two young boys. Its sides were dented and warped from use, but its grapples were still strong and powerful. In addition to the usual reinforced plates across its nose there was a gouge of tough steel, a jutting jaw that was already sliding into position, ready and able.

Mecho-Products, its manufacturer, had lavished attention on this jaw-construction. It was their trademark, their unique feature. Their ads, their brochures, stressed the massive frontal scoop mounted on all their models. And there was an optional assist: a cutting edge, power-driven, that at extra cost could easily be installed in their "Luxury-line" models.

This blue Nanny was so equipped.

Moving cautiously ahead, the blue Nanny reached the fence. It stopped and carefully inspected the boards. They were thin and rotted, put up a long time ago. It pushed its hard head against the wood. The fence gave, splintering and ripping. At once the green Nanny rose on its back treads, its grapples leaping out. A fierce joy filled it, a bursting excitement. The wild frenzy of battle.

The two closed, rolling silently on the ground, their grapples locked. Neither made any noise, the blue Mecho-Products Nanny nor the smaller, lighter, pale-green Service Industries, Inc., Nanny. On and on they fought, hugged tightly together, the great jaw trying to push underneath, into the soft treads. And the green Nanny trying to hook its metal point into the eyes that gleamed fitfully against its side. The green Nanny had the disadvantage of being a medium-priced model; it was outclassed and outweighed. But it fought grimly, furiously.

On and on they struggled, rolling in the wet soil. Without sound of any kind. Performing the wrathful, ultimate task for which each had been designed.

"I can't imagine," Mary Fields murmured, shaking her head. "I just don't know."

"Do you suppose some animal did it?" Tom conjectured. "Are there any big dogs in the neighborhood?"

"No. There was a big red Irish setter, but they moved away, to the country. That was Mr. Petty's dog."

The two of them watched, troubled and disturbed. Nanny lay at rest by the bathroom door, watching Bobby to make sure he brushed his teeth. The green hull was twisted and bent. One eye had been shattered, the glass knocked out, splintered. One grapple no longer retracted completely; it hung forlornly out of its little door, dragging uselessly.

"I just don't understand," Mary repeated. "I'll call the repair place and see what they say. Tom, it must have happened sometime during the night. While we were asleep. The noises I heard—"

"Shhh," Tom muttered warningly. Nanny was coming

toward them, away from the bathroom. Clicking and whirring raggedly, she passed them, a limping green tub of metal that emitted an unrhythmic, grating sound. Tom and Mary Fields unhappily watched her as she lumbered slowly into the living room.

"I wonder," Mary murmured.

"Wonder what?"

"I wonder if this will happen again." She glanced up suddenly at her husband, eyes full of worry. "You know how the children love her . . . and they need her so. They just wouldn't be safe without her. Would they?"

"Maybe it won't happen again," Tom said soothingly. "Maybe it was an accident." But he didn't believe it; he knew better. What had happened was no accident.

From the garage he backed his surface cruiser, maneuvered it until its loading entrance was locked against the rear door of the house. It took only a moment to load the sagging, dented Nanny inside; within ten minutes he was on his way across town to the repair and maintenance department of Service Industries, Inc.

The serviceman, in grease-stained white overalls, met him at the entrance. "Troubles?" he asked wearily; behind him, in the depths of the block-long building, stood rows of battered Nannies, in various stages of disassembly. "What seems to be the matter this time?"

Tom said nothing. He ordered the Nanny out of the cruiser and waited while the serviceman examined it for himself.

Shaking his head, the serviceman crawled to his feet and wiped grease from his hands. "That's going to run into money," he said. "The whole neural transmission's out."

His throat dry, Tom demanded: "Ever seen anything like this before? It didn't break; you know that. It was demolished."

"Sure," the serviceman agreed tonelessly. "It pretty much got taken down a peg. On the basis of those missing chunks—" He indicated the dented anterior hull-sections. "I'd guess it was one of Mecho's new jaw-models."

Tom Fields's blood stopped moving in his veins. "Then this isn't new to you," he said softly, his chest constricting. "This goes on all the time."

"Well, Mecho just put out that jaw-model. It's not half bad . . . costs about twice what this model ran. Of course," the serviceman added thoughtfully, "we have an equivalent. We can match their best, and for less money."

Keeping his voice as calm as possible, Tom said: "I want this one fixed. I'm not getting another."

"I'll do what I can. But it won't be the same as it was. The damage goes pretty deep. I'd advise you to trade it in—you can get damn near what you paid. With the new models coming out in a month or so, the salesmen are eager as hell to—"

"Let me get this straight." Shakily, Tom Fields lit up a cigarette. "You people really don't want to fix these, do you? You want to sell brand-new ones, when these break down." He eyed the repairman intently. "Break down, or are *knocked* down."

The repairman shrugged. "It seems like a waste of time to fix it up. It's going to get finished off, anyhow, soon." He kicked the misshapen green hull with his boot. "This model is around three years old. Mister, it's obsolete."

"Fix it up," Tom grated. He was beginning to see the whole picture; his self-control was about to snap. "I'm not getting a new one! I want this one fixed!"

"Sure," the serviceman said, resigned. He began making out a work-order sheet. "We'll do our best. But don't expect miracles."

While Tom Fields was jerkily signing his name to the sheet, two more damaged Nannies were brought into the repair building.

"When can I get it back?" he demanded.

"It'll take a couple of days," the mechanic said, nodding toward the rows of semi-repaired Nannies behind him. "As you can see," he added leisurely, "we're pretty well full-up."

"I'll wait," Tom said tautly. "Even if it takes a month."

"Let's go to the park!" Jean cried.

So they went to the park.

It was a lovely day, with the sun shining down hotly and the grass and flowers blowing in the wind. The two children strolled along the gravel path, breathing the warm-scented air, taking deep breaths and holding the presence of roses and hydrangeas and orange blossoms inside them as long as possible. They passed through a swaying grove of dark, rich cedars. The ground was soft with mold underfoot, the velvet, moist fur of a living world beneath their feet. Beyond the cedars, where the sun returned and the blue sky flashed back into being, a great green lawn stretched out.

Behind them Nanny came, trudging slowly, her treads clicking noisily. The dragging grapple had been repaired, and a new optic unit had been installed in place of the damaged one. But the smooth coordination of the old days was lacking; and the clean-cut lines of her hull had not been restored. Occasionally she halted, and the two children halted, too, waiting impatiently for her to catch up with them.

"What's the matter, Nanny?" Bobby asked her.

"Something's wrong with her," Jean complained. "She's been all funny since last Wednesday. Real slow and funny. And she was gone, for awhile."

"She was in the repair shop," Bobby announced. "I guess she got sort of tired. She's old, Daddy says. I heard him and Mommy talking."

A little sadly they continued on, with Nanny painfully following. Now they had come to benches placed here and there on the lawn, with people languidly dozing in the sun. On the grass lay a young man, a newspaper over his face, his coat rolled up under his head. They crossed carefully around him, so as not to step on him.

"There's the lake!" Jean shouted, her spirits returning.

The great field of grass sloped gradually down, lower and lower. At the far end, the lowest end, lay a path, a gravel trail, and beyond that, a blue lake. The two children scampered excitedly, filled with ancitipation. They hurried faster and faster down the carefully-graded slope, Nanny struggling miserably to keep up with them.

"The lake!"

"Last one there's a dead Martian stinko-bug!"

Breathlessly, they rushed across the path, onto the tiny strip of green bank against which the water lapped. Bobby threw himself down on his hands and knees, laughing and panting and peering down into the water. Jean settled down beside him, smoothing her dress tidily into place.

Deep in the cloudy-blue water some tadpoles and minnows moved, minute artificial fish too small to catch.

At one end of the lake some children were floating boats with flapping white sails. At a bench a fat man sat laboriously reading a book, a pipe jammed in his mouth. A young man and woman strolled along the edge of the lake together, arm in arm, intent on each other, oblivious of the world around them.

"I wish we had a boat," Bobby said wistfully.

Grinding and clashing, Nanny managed to make her way across the path and up to them. She stopped, settling down, retracting her treads. She did not stir. One eye, the good eye, reflected the sunlight. The other had not been synchronized; it gaped with futile emptiness. She had managed to shift most of her weight on her less-damaged side, but her motion was bad and uneven, and slow. There was a smell about her, an odor of burning oil and friction.

Jean studied her. Finally she patted the bent green side sympathetically. "Poor Nanny! What did you do, Nanny? What happened to you? Were you in a wreck?"

"Let's push Nanny in," Bobby said lazily. "And see if she can swim. Can a Nanny swim?"

Jean said no, because she was too heavy. She would sink to the bottom and they would never see her again.

"Then we won't push her in," Bobby agreed.

For a time there was silence. Overhead a few birds fluttered past, plump specks streaking swiftly across the sky. A small boy on a bicycle came riding hesitantly along the gravel path, his front wheel wobbling.

"I wish I had a bicycle," Bobby murmured.

The boy careened on past. Across the lake the fat man stood up and knocked his pipe against the bench. He closed his book and sauntered off along the path, wiping his perspiring forehead with a vast red handkerchief.

"What happens to Nannies when they get old?" Bobby asked wonderingly. "What do they do? Where do they go?"

"They go to heaven." Jean lovingly thumped the green dented hull with her hand. "Just like everybody else."

"Are Nannies born? Were there always Nannies?" Bobby had begun to conjecture on ultimate cosmic mysteries. "Maybe there was a time before there were Nannies. I wonder what the world was like in the days before Nannies lived."

"Of course there were always Nannies," Jean said impatiently. "If there weren't, where did they come from?"

Bobby couldn't answer that. He meditated for a time, but presently he became sleepy . . . he was really too young to solve such problems. His eyelids became heavy and he yawned. Both he and Jean lay on the warm grass by the edge of the lake, watching the sky and the clouds, listening to the wind moving through the grove of cedar trees. Beside them the battered green Nanny rested and recuperated her meager strength.

A little girl came slowly across the field of grass, a pretty child in a blue dress with a bright ribbon in her long dark hair. She was coming toward the lake.

"Look," Jean said. "There's Phyllis Casworthy. She has an *orange* Nanny."

They watched, interested. "Who ever heard of an orange Nanny?" Bobby said, disgusted. The girl and her Nanny crossed the path a short distance down, and reached the edge of the lake. She and her orange Nanny halted, gazing around at the water and the white sails of toy boats, the mechanical fish.

"Her Nanny is bigger than ours," Jean observed.

"That's true," Bobby admitted. He thumped the green side loyally. "But ours is nicer. Isn't she?"

Their Nanny did not move. Surprised, he turned to look. The green Nanny stood rigid, taut. Its better eye stalk was far out, staring at the orange Nanny fixedly, unwinkingly.

"What's the matter?" Bobby asked uncomfortably.

"Nanny, what's the matter?" Jean echoed.

The green Nanny whirred, as its gears meshed. Its treads dropped and locked into place with a sharp metallic snap. Slowly its doors retracted and its grapples slithered out.

"Nanny, what are you doing?" Jean scrambled nervously to her feet. Bobby leaped up, too.

"Nanny! What's going on?"

"Let's go." Jean said, frightened. "Let's go home."

"Come on, Nanny," Bobby ordered. "We're going home, now."

The green Nanny moved away from them; it was totally unaware of their existence. Down the lake-side the other Nanny, the great orange Nanny, detached itself from the little girl and began to flow.

"Nanny, you come back!" the little girl's voice came, shrill and apprehensive.

Jean and Bobby rushed up the sloping lawn, away from the lake. "She'll come!" Bobby said. "Nanny! Please come!"

But the Nanny did not come.

The orange Nanny neared. It was huge, much more immense than the blue Mecho jaw-model that had come into the back yard that night. That one now lay scattered in pieces on the far side of the fence, hull ripped open, its parts strewn everywhere.

This Nanny was the largest the green Nanny had ever seen. The green Nanny moved awkwardly to meet it, raising its grapples and preparing its internal shields. But the orange Nanny was unbending a square arm of metal, mounted on a long cable. The metal arm whipped out, rising high in the air. It began to whirl in a circle, gathering ominous velocity, faster and faster.

The green Nanny hesitated. It retreated, moving uncertainly away from the swinging mace of metal. And as it rested warily, unhappily, trying to make up its mind, the other leaped.

"Nanny!" Jean screamed.

"Nanny! Nanny!"

The two metal bodies rolled furiously in the grass, fighting and struggling desperately. Again and again the metal mace came, bashing wildly into the green side. The warm sun shone benignly down on them. The surface of the lake eddied gently in the wind.

"Nanny!" Bobby screamed, helplessly jumping up and down.

But there was no response from the frenzied, twisting mass of crashing orange and green.

"What are you going to do?" Mary Fields asked, tight-lipped and pale.

"You stay here." Tom grabbed up his coat and threw it on; he yanked his hat down from the closet shelf and strode toward the front door.

"Where are you going?"

"Is the cruiser out front?" Tom pulled open the front door and made his way out onto the porch. The two children, miserable and trembling, watched him fearfully.

"Yes," Mary murmured, "it's out front. But where—"

Tom turned abruptly to the children. "You're sure she's—*dead?*"

Bobby nodded. His face was streaked with grimy tears. "Pieces . . . all over the lawn."

Tom nodded grimly. "I'll be right back. And don't worry at all. You three stay here."

He strode down the front steps, down the walk, to the parked cruiser. A moment later they heard him drive furiously away.

He had to go to several agencies before he found what he wanted. Service Industries had nothing he could use; he was through with them. It was at Allied Domestic that he saw exactly what he was looking for, displayed in their luxurious, well-lighted window. They were just closing, but the clerk let him inside when he saw the expression on his face.

"I'll take it," Tom said, reaching into his coat for his checkbook.

"Which one, sir?" the clerk faltered.

"The big one. The big black one in the window. With the four arms and the ram in front."

The clerk beamed, his face aglow with pleasure. "Yes sir!" he cried, whipping out his order pad. "The Imperator Delux, with power-beam focus. Did you want the optional high-velocity grapple-lock and the remote-control feedback? At moderate cost, we can equip her with a visual report screen; you can follow the situation from the comfort of your own living room."

"The situation?" Tom said thickly.

"As she goes into action." The clerk began writing rapidly. "And I mean *action*—this model warms up and closes in on its adversary within fifteen seconds of the time its activated. You can't find faster reaction in any single-unit models, ours or anybody else's. Six months ago, they said fifteen second closing was a pipe dream." The clerk laughed excitedly. "But science strides on."

A strange cold numbness settled over Tom Fields. "Listen," he said hoarsely. Grabbing the clerk by the lapel he yanked him closer. The order pad fluttered away; the clerk gulped with surprise and fright. "Listen to me," Tom grated, "you're building these things bigger all the time—*aren't you?* Every year, new models, new weapons. You and all the other companies—building them with improved equipment to destroy each other."

"Oh," the clerk squeaked indignantly, "Allied Domestic's models are *never* destroyed. Banged up a little now and then, perhaps, but you show me one of our models that's been put out of commission." With dignity, he retrieved his order pad and smoothed down his coat. "No, sir," he said emphatically, "our models survive. Why, I saw a seven-year-old Allied running around, an old Model 3-S. Dented a bit, perhaps, but plenty of fire left. I'd like to see one of those cheap Protecto-Corp. models try to tangle with *that.*"

Controlling himself with an effort, Tom asked: "But why? What's it all for? What's the purpose in this—competition between them?"

The clerk hesitated. Uncertainly, he began again with his order pad. "Yes sir," he said. "Competition; you put your finger right on it. Successful competition, to be exact. Allied Domestic doesn't meet competition—it *demolishes* it."

It took a second for Tom Fields to react. Then understanding came. "I see," he said. "In other words, every year these things are obsolete. No good, not large enough. Not powerful enough. And if they're not replaced, if I don't get a new one, a more advanced model—"

"Your present Nanny was, ah, the loser?" The clerk smiled knowingly. "Your present model was, perhaps, slightly anachronistic? It failed to meet present-day standards of competition? It, ah, failed to come out at the end of the day?"

"It never came home," Tom said thickly.

"Yes, it was demolished . . . I fully understand. Very common. You see, sir, you don't have a choice. It's nobody's fault, sir. Don't blame us; don't blame Allied Domestic."

"But," Tom said harshly, "when one is destroyed, that means you sell another one. That means a sale for you. Money in the cash register."

"True. But we all have to meet contemporary standards of excellence. We can't let ourselves fall behind . . . as you saw, sir, if you don't mind my saying so, you saw the unfortunate consequences of falling behind."

"Yes," Tom agreed, in an almost inaudible voice. "They told me not to have her repaired. They said I should replace her."

The clerk's confident, smugly-beaming face seemed to expand. Like a miniature sun, it glowed happily, exaltedly. "But now you're all set up, sir. With this model you're right up there in the front. Your worries are over, Mr. . . ." He halted expectantly. "Your name, sir? To whom shall I make out this purchase order?"

Bobby and Jean watched with fascination as the delivery men lugged the enormous crate into the living room. Grunting and sweating, they set it down and straightened gratefully up.

"All right," Tom said crisply. "Thanks."

"Not at all, mister." The delivery men stalked out, noisily closing the door after them.

"Daddy, what is it?" Jean whispered. The two children came cautiously around the crate, wide-eyed and awed.

"You'll see in a minute."

"Tom, it's past their bedtime," Mary protested. "Can't they look at it tomorrow?"

"I want them to look at it *now*." Tom disappeared downstairs into the basement and returned with a screwdriver. Kneeling on the floor beside the crate he began rapidly unscrewing the bolts that held it together. "They can go to bed a little late, for once."

He removed the boards, one by one, working expertly and calmly. At last the final board was gone, propped up against the wall with the others. He unclipped the book of instructions and the 90-day warranty and handed them to Mary. "Hold onto these."

"It's a Nanny!" Bobby cried.

"It's a huge, huge Nanny!"

In the crate the great black shape lay quietly, like an enormous metal tortoise, encased in a coating of grease. Carefully checked, oiled, and fully guaranteed. Tom nodded. "That's right. It's a Nanny, a new Nanny. To take the place of the old one."

"For *us?*"

"Yes." Tom sat down in a nearby chair and lit a cigarette. "Tomorrow morning we'll turn her on and warm her up. See how she runs."

The children's eyes were like saucers. Neither of them could breathe or speak.

"But this time," Mary said, "you must stay away from the park. Don't take her near the park. You hear?"

"No," Tom contradicted. "They can go in the park."

Mary glanced uncertainly at him. "But that orange thing might—"

Tom smiled grimly. "It's fine with me if they go into the park." He leaned toward Bobby and Jean. "You kids go into the park any time you want. And don't be afraid of anything. Of anything or anyone. Remember that."

He kicked the end of the massive crate with his toe. "There isn't anything in the world you have to be afraid of. Not anymore."

Bobby and Jean nodded, still gazing fixedly into the crate.

"All right, Daddy," Jean breathed.

"Boy, look at her!" Bobby whispered. "Just look at her! I can hardly wait till tomorrow!"

Mrs. Andrew Casworthy greeted her husband on the front steps of their attractive three-story house, wringing her hands anxiously.

"What's the matter?" Casworthy grunted, taking off his hat. With his pocket handkerchief he wiped sweat from his florid face. "Lord, it was hot today. What's wrong? What is it?"

"Andrew, I'm afraid—"

"What the hell happened?"

"Phyllis came home from the park today without her Nanny. She was bent and scratched yesterday when Phyllis brought her home, and Phyllis is so upset I can't make out—"

"Without her Nanny?"

"She came home alone. By herself. All alone."

Slow rage suffused the man's heavy features. "What happened?"

"Something in the park, like yesterday. Something attacked her Nanny. Destroyed her! I can't get the story exactly straight, but something black, something huge and black . . . it must have been another Nanny."

Casworthy's jaw slowly jutted out. His thickset face turned ugly dark red, a deep unwholesome flush that rose ominously and settled in place. Abruptly, he turned on his heel.

"Where are you going?" his wife fluttered nervously.

The paunchy, red-faced man stalked rapidly down the walk toward his sleek surface cruiser, already reaching for the door handle.

"I'm going to shop for another Nanny," he muttered. "The best damn Nanny I can get. Even if I have to go to a hundred stores. I want the best—and the biggest."

"But, dear," his wife began, hurrying apprehensively after him, "can we really afford it?" Wringing her hands together anxiously, she raced on: "I mean, wouldn't it be better to wait? Until you've had time to think it over, perhaps. Maybe later on, when you're a little more—calm."

But Andrew Casworthy wasn't listening. Already the surface cruiser boiled with quick, eager life, ready to leap forward. "Nobody's going to get ahead of me," he said grimly, his heavy lips twitching. "I'll show them, all of them. Even if I have to get a new size designed. Even if I have to get one of those manufacturers to turn out a new model for me!"

And, oddly, he knew one of them would.

THE TURNING WHEEL

BARD CHAI said thoughtfully, "Cults." He examined a tape-report grinding from the receptor. The receptor was rusty and unoiled; it whined piercingly and sent up an acrid wisp of smoke. Chai shut it off as its pitted surface began to heat ugly red. Presently he finished with the tape and tossed it with a heap of refuse jamming the mouth of a disposal slot.

"What about cults?" Bard Sung-wu asked faintly. He brought himself back with an effort, and forced a smile of interest on his plump olive-yellow face. "You were saying?"

"Any stable society is menaced by cults; our society is no exception." Chai rubbed his finely-tapered fingers together reflectively. "Certain lower strata are axiomatically dissatisfied. Their hearts burn with envy of those the wheel has placed above them; in secret they form fanatic, rebellious bands. They meet in the dark of the night; they insidiously express inversions of accepted norms; they delight in flaunting basic mores and customs."

"Ugh," Sung-wu agreed. "I mean," he explained quickly, "it seems incredible people could practice such fanatic and disgusting rites." He got nervously to his feet. "I must go, if it's permitted."

"Wait," snapped Chai. "You are familiar with the Detroit area?"

Uneasily, Sung-wu nodded. "Very slightly."

With characteristic vigor, Chai made his decision. "I'm sending you; investigate and make a blue-slip report. If this group is dangerous, the Holy Arm should know. It's of the worst elements—the Techno class." He made a wry face. "Caucasians, hulking, hairy things. We'll give you six months in Spain, on your return; you can poke over ruins of abandoned cities."

"Caucasians!" Sung-wu exclaimed, his face turning green. "But I haven't been well; please, if somebody else could go—"

"You, perhaps, hold to the Broken Feather theory?" Chai raised an eyebrow. "An amazing philologist, Broken Feather; I took partial instruction from him. He held, you know, the Caucasian to be descended of Neanderthal stock. Their extreme size, thick body hair, their general brutish cast, reveal an innate inability to comprehend anything but a purely animalistic horizontal; proselytism is a waste of time."

He affixed the younger man with a stern eye. "I wouldn't send you, if I didn't have unusual faith in your devotion."

Sung-wu fingered his beads miserably. "Elron be praised," he muttered; "you are too kind."

Sung-wu slid into a lift and was raised, amid great groans and whirrings and false stops, to the top level of the Central Chamber building. He hurried down a corridor dimly lit by occasional yellow bulbs. A moment later he approached the doors of the scanning offices and flashed his identification at the robot guard. "Is Bard Feip'ang within?" he inquired.

"Verily," the robot answered, stepping aside.

Sung-wu entered the offices, bypassed the rows of rusted, discarded machines, and entered the still-functioning wing. He located his brother-in-law, hunched over some graphs at one of the desks, laboriously copying material by hand. "Clearness be with you," Sung-wu murmured.

Fei-p'ang glanced up in annoyance. "I told you not to come again; if the Arm finds out I'm letting you use the scanner for a personal plot, they'll stretch me on the rack."

"Gently," Sung-wu murmured, his hand on his relation's shoulder. "This is the last time. I'm going away; one more look, a final look." His olive face took on a pleading, piteous cast. "The turn comes for me very soon; this will be our last conversation."

Sung-wu's piteous look hardened into cunning. "You

wouldn't want it on your soul; no restitution will be possible at this late date."

Fei-p'ang snorted. "All right; but for Elron's sake, do it quickly."

Sung-wu hurried to the mother-scanner and seated himself in the rickety basket. He snapped on the controls, clamped his forehead to the viewpiece, inserted his identity tab, and set the space-time finger into motion. Slowly, reluctantly, the ancient mechanism coughed into life and began tracing his personal tab along the future track.

Sung-wu's hands shook; his body trembled; sweat dripped from his neck, as he saw himself scampering in miniature. *Poor Sung-wu,* he thought wretchedly. The mite of a thing hurried about its duties; this was but eight months hence. Harried and beset, it performed its tasks—and then, in a subsequent continuum, fell down and died.

Sung-wu removed his eyes from the viewpiece and waited for his pulse to slow. He could stand that part, watching the moment of death; it was what came next that was too jangling for him.

He breathed a silent prayer. Had he fasted enough? In the four-day purge and self-flagellation, he had used the whip with metal points, the heaviest possible. He had given away all his money; he had smashed a lovely vase his mother had left him, a treasured heirloom; he had rolled in the filth and mud in the center of town. Hundreds had seen him. Now, surely, all this was enough. But time was so short!

Faint courage stirring, he sat up and again put his eyes to the viewpiece. He was shaking with terror. What if it hadn't changed? What if his mortification weren't enough? He spun the controls, sending the finger tracing his time-track past the moment of death.

Sung-wu shrieked and scrambled back in horror. His future was the same, exactly the same; there had been no change at all. His guilt had been too great to be washed away in such short a time; it would take ages—and he didn't have ages.

He left the scanner and passed by his brother-in-law. "Thanks," he muttered shakily.

For once, a measure of compassion touched Fei-p'ang's

efficient brown features. "Bad news? The next turn brings an unfortunate manifestation?"

"Bad scarcely describes it."

Fei-p'ang's pity turned to righteous rebuke. "Who do you have to blame but yourself?" he demanded sternly. "You know your conduct in this manifestation determines the next; if you look forward to a future life as a lower animal, it should make you glance over your behavior and repent your wrongs. The cosmic law that governs us is impartial. It is true justice: cause and effect; what you do determines what you next become—there can be no blame and no sorrow. There can be only understanding and repentence." His curiosity overcame him. "What is it? A snake? A squirrel?"

"It's no affair of yours," Sung-wu said, as he moved unhappily toward the exit doors.

"I'll look myself."

"Go ahead." Sung-wu pushed moodily out into the hall. He was dazed with despair: it hadn't changed; it was still the same.

In eight months he would die, stricken by one of the numerous plagues that swept over the inhabited parts of the world. He would become feverish, break out with red spots, turn and twist in an anguish of delirium. His bowels would drop out; his flesh would waste away; his eyes would roll up; and after an interminable time of suffering, he would die. His body would lie in a mass heap, with hundreds of others—a whole streetful of dead, to be carted away by one of the robot sweepers, happily immune. His mortal remains would be burned in a common rubbish incinerator at the outskirts of the city.

Meanwhile, the eternal spark, Sung-wu's divine soul, would hurry from this space-time manifestation to the next in order. But it would not rise; it would sink; he had watched its descent on the scanner many times. There was always the same hideous picture—a sight beyond endurance—of his soul, as it plummeted down like a stone, into one of the lowest continua, a sinkhole of a manifestation at the very bottom of the ladder.

He had sinned. In his youth, Sung-wu had got mixed up with a black-eyed wench with long flowing hair, a glittering waterfall down her back and shoulders. Inviting red lips, plump breasts, hips that undulated and beckoned unmistakably. She was the wife of a friend, from the Warrior class, but he had taken her as his mistress; he had been *certain* time remained to rectify his venality.

But he was wrong: the wheel was soon to turn for him. The plague—not enough time to fast and pray and do good works. He was determined to go down, straight down to a wallowing, foul-aired planet in a stinking red-sun system, an ancient pit of filth and decay and unending slime—a jungle world of the lowest type.

In it, he would be a shiny-winged fly, a great blue-bottomed, buzzing carrion-eater that hummed and guzzled and crawled through the rotting carcasses of great lizards, slain in combat.

From this swamp, this pest-ridden planet in a diseased, contaminated system, he would have to rise painfully up the endless rungs of the cosmic ladder he had already climbed. It had taken eons to climb this far, to the level of a human being on the planet Earth, in the bright yellow Sol system; now he would have to do it all over again.

Chai beamed, "Elron be with you," as the corroded observation ship was checked by the robot crew, and finally okayed for limited flight. Sung-wu slowly entered the ship and seated himself at what remained of the controls. He waved listlessly, then slammed the lock and bolted it by hand.

As the ship limped into the late afternoon sky, he reluctantly consulted the reports and records Chai had transferred to him.

The Tinkerists were a small cult; they claimed only a few hundred members, all drawn from the Techno class, which was the most despised of the social castes. The Bards, of course, were at the top; they were the teachers of society, the holy men who guided man to clearness. Then the Poets; they turned into saga the great legends of Elron Hu, who lived (according to legend) in the hideous days of the Time of Madness. Below the Poets were the Artists; then the Musicians; then the Workers, who supervised the robot crews. After them the Businessmen, the Warriors, the Farmers, and finally, at the bottom, the Technos.

Most of the Technos were Caucasians—immense white-skinned things, incredibly hairy, like apes; their resemblance to the great apes was striking. Perhaps Broken Feather was right; perhaps they did have Neanderthal blood and were outside the possibility of clearness. Sung-wu had always considered himself an anti-racist; he disliked those who maintained the Caucasians were a race apart. Extremists believed eternal damage would result to the species if the Caucasians were allowed to intermarry.

In any case, the problem was academic; no decent, self-respecting woman of the higher classes—of Indian or Mongolian, or Bantu stock—would allow herself to be approached by a *Cauc*.

Below his ship, the barren countryside spread out, ugly and bleak. Great red spots that hadn't yet been overgrown, and slag surfaces were still visible—but by this time most ruins were covered by soil and crabgrass. He could see men and robots farming; villages, countless tiny brown circles in the green fields; occasional ruins of ancient cities—gaping sores like blind mouths, eternally open to the sky. They would never close, not now.

Ahead was the Detroit area, named, so it ran, for some now-forgotten spiritual leader. There were more villages, here. Off to his left, the leaden surface of a body of water, a lake of some kind. Beyond that—only Elron knew. No one went that far; there was no human life there, only wild animals and deformed things spawned from radiation infestation still lying heavy in the north.

He dropped his ship down. An open field lay to his right; a robot farmer was plowing with a metal hook welded to its waist, a section torn off some discarded machine. It stopped dragging the hook and gazed up in amazement, as Sung-wu landed the ship awkwardly and bumped to a halt.

"Clearness be with you," the robot rasped obediently, as Sung-wu climbed out.

Sung-wu gathered up his bundle of reports and papers and stuffed them in a briefcase. He snapped the ship's lock and hurried off toward the ruins of the city. The robot went back to dragging the rusty metal hook through the hard ground, its pitted body bent double with the strain, working slowly, silently, uncomplaining.

The little boy piped, "Whither, Bard?" as Sung-wu pushed wearily through the tangled debris and slag. He was a little black-faced Bantu, in red rags sewed and patched together. He ran alongside Sung-wu like a puppy, leaping and bounding and grinning white-teethed.

Sung-wu became immediately crafty; his intrigue with the black-haired girl had taught him elemental dodges and evasions. "My ship broke down," he answered cautiously; it was certainly common enough. "It was the last ship still in operation at our field."

The boy skipped and laughed and broke off bits of green weeds that grew along the trail. "I know somebody who can fix it," he cried carelessly.

Sung-wu's pulse-rate changed. "Oh?" he murmured, as if uninterested. "There are those around here who practice the questionable art of repairing."

The boy nodded solemnly.

"Technos?" Sung-wu pursued. "Are there many of them here, around these old ruins?"

More black-faced boys, and some little dark-eyed Bantu girls, came scampering through the slag and ruins. "What's the matter with your ship?" one hollered at Sung-wu. "Won't it run?"

They all ran and shouted around him, as he advanced slowly—an unusually wild bunch, completely undisciplined. They rolled and fought and tumbled and chased each other around madly.

"How many of you," Sung-wu demanded, "have taken your first instruction?"

There was a sudden uneasy silence. The children looked at each other guiltily; none of them answered.

"Good Elron!" Sung-wu exclaimed in horror. "Are you all untaught?"

Heads hung guiltily.

"How do you expect to phase yourselves with the cosmic will? How can you expect to know the divine plan? This is really too much!"

He pointed a plump finger at one of the boys. "Are you constantly preparing yourself for the life to come? Are you constantly purging and purifying yourself? Do you deny yourself meat, sex, entertainment, financial gain, education, leisure?"

But it was obvious; their unrestrained laughter and play proved they were still jangled, far from clear— And clearness is the only road by which a person can gain understanding of the eternal plan, the cosmic wheel which turns endlessly, for all living things.

"Butterflies!" Sung-wu snorted with disgust. "You are no better than the beasts and birds of the field, who take no heed of the morrow. You play and game for today, thinking tomorrow won't come. Like insects—"

But the thought of insects reminded him of the shiny-winged blue-rumped fly, creeping over a rotting lizard carcass, and Sung-wu's stomach did a flip-flop; he forced it back in place and strode on, toward the line of villages emerging ahead.

Farmers were working the barren fields on all sides. A thin layer of soil over slag; a few limp wheat stalks waved, thin and emaciated. The ground was terrible, the worst he had seen. He could feel the metal under his feet; it was almost to the surface. Bent men and women watered their sickly crops with tin cans, old metal containers picked from the ruins. An ox was pulling a crude cart.

In another field, women were weeding by hand; all moved slowly, stupidly, victims of hookworm, from the soil. They were all barefoot. The children hadn't picked it up yet, but they soon would.

Sung-wu gazed up at the sky and gave thanks to Elron; here, suffering was unusually severe; trials of exceptional vividness lay on every hand. These men and women were being tempered in a hot crucible; their souls were probably purified to an astonishing degree. A baby lay in the shade, beside a half-dozing mother. Flies crawled over its eyes; its mother breathed heavily, hoarsely, her mouth open. An unhealthy flush discolored her brown cheeks. Her belly bulged; she was already pregnant again. Another eternal soul to be raised from a lower level. Her great breasts sagged and wobbled as she stirred in her sleep, spilling out over her dirty wraparound.

"Come here," Sung-wu called sharply to the gang of black-faced children who followed along after him. "I'm going to talk to you."

The children approached, eyes on the ground, and assembled in a silent circle around him. Sung-wu sat down, placed his briefcase beside him and folded his legs expertly under him in the traditional posture outlined by Elron in his seventh book of teaching.

"I will ask and you will answer," Sung-wu stated. "You know the basic catechisms?" He peered sharply around. "Who knows the basic catechisms?"

One or two hands went up. Most of the children looked away unhappily.

"First!" snapped Sung-wu. *"Who are you?* You are a minute fragment of the cosmic plan.

"Second! *What are you?* A mere speck in a system so vast as to be beyond comprehension.

"Third! *What is the way of life?* To fulfill what is required by the cosmic forces

"Fourth! *Where are you?* On one step of the cosmic ladder.

"Fifth! *Where have you been?* Through endless steps; each turn of the wheel advances or depresses you.

"Sixth! *What determines your direction at the next turn?* Your conduct in this manifestation.

"Seventh! *What is right conduct?* Submitting yourself to the eternal forces, the cosmic elements that make up the divine plan.

"Eighth! *What is the significance of suffering?* To purify the soul.

"Ninth! *What is the significance of death?* To release the person from this manifestation, so he may rise to a new rung of the ladder.

"Tenth—"

But at that moment Sung-wu broke off. Two quasi-human shapes were approaching him. Immense white-skinned figures striding across the baked fields, between the sickly rows of wheat.

Technos—coming to meet him; his flesh crawled. Caucs. Their skins glittered pale and unhealthy, like nocturnal insects, dug from under rocks.

He rose to his feet, conquered his disgust, and prepared to greet them.

Sung-wu said, "Clearness!" He could smell them, a musky sheep smell, as they came to a halt in front of him. Two bucks, two immense sweating males, skin damp and sticky, with beards, and long disorderly hair. They wore sailcloth trousers and boots. With horror Sung-wu perceived a thick body-hair, on their chests, like woven mats—tufts in their armpits, on their arms, wrists, even the backs of their hands. Maybe Broken Feather was right; perhaps, in these great lumbering blond-haired beasts, the archaic Neanderthal stock—the false men—still survived. He could almost see the ape, peering from behind their blue eyes.

"Hi," the first Cauc said. After a moment he added reflectively, "My name's Jamison."

"Pete Ferris," the other grunted. Neither of them observed the customary deferences; Sung-wu winced but managed not to show it. Was it deliberate, a veiled insult, or perhaps mere ignorance? This was hard to tell; in lower classes there was, as Chai said, an ugly undercurrent of resentment and envy, and hostility.

"I'm making a routine survey," Sung-wu explained, "on birth and death rates in rural areas. I'll be here a few days. Is there some place I can stay? Some public inn or hostel?"

The two Cauc bucks were silent. "Why?" one of them demanded bluntly.

Sung-wu blinked. "Why? Why what?"

"Why are you making a survey? If you want any information we'll supply it."

Sung-wu was incredulous. "Do you know to whom you're talking? I'm a Bard! Why, you're ten classes down; how dare you—" He choked with rage. In these rural areas the Technos had utterly forgotten their place. What was ailing the local Bards? Were they letting the system break apart?

He shuddered violently at the thought of what it would mean if Technos and Farmers and Businessmen were allowed to intermingle—even intermarry, and eat, and drink, in the same places. The whole structure of society would collpase. If all were to ride the same carts, use the same outhouses; it passed belief. A sudden nightmare picture loomed up before Sung-wu, of Technos living and mating with women of the Bard and Poet classes. He visioned a horizontally-oriented society, all persons on the same level, with horror. It went against the very grain of the cosmos, against the divine plan; it was the Time of Madness all over again. He shuddered.

"Where is the Manager of this area?" he demanded. "Take me to him; I'll deal directly with him."

The two Caucs turned and headed back the way they had come, without a word. After a moment of fury, Sung-wu followed behind them.

They led him through withered fields and over barren, eroded hills on which nothing grew; the ruins increased. At the edge of the city, a line of meager villages had been set up; he saw leaning, rickety wood huts, and mud streets. From the villages a thick stench rose, the smell of offal and death.

Doga lay sleeping under the huts; children poked and played in the filth and rotting debris. A few old people sat on porches, vacant-faced, eyes glazed and dull. Chickens pecked around, and he saw pigs and skinny cats—and the eternal rusting piles of metal, sometimes thirty feet high. Great towers of red slag were heaped up everywhere.

Beyond the villages were the ruins proper—endless miles of abandoned wreckage; skeletons of buildings; concrete walls; bathtubs and pipe; overturned wrecks that had been cars. All these were from the Time of Madness, the decade that had finally rung the curtain down on the sorriest interval in man's history. The five centuries of madness and jangledness were now known as the Age of Heresy, when man had gone against the divine plan and taken his destiny in his own hands.

They came to a larger hut, a two-story wood structure. The Caucs climbed a decaying flight of steps; boards creaked and gave ominously under their heavy boots. Sung-wu followed them nervously; they came out on a porch, a kind of open balcony.

On the balcony sat a man, an obese copper-skinned official in unbuttoned breeches, his shiny black hair pulled back and tied with a bone against his bulging red neck. His nose was large and prominent, his face, flat and wide, with many chins. He was drinking lime juice from a tin cup and gazing down at the mud street below. As the two Caucs appeared he rose slightly, a prodigious effort.

"This man," the Cauc named Jamison said, indicating Sung-wu, "wants to see you."

Sung-wu pushed angrily forward. "I am a Bard, from the Central Chamber; do you people recognize *this?*" He tore open his robe and flashed the symbol of the Holy Arm, gold worked to form a swath of flaming red. "I insist you accord me proper treatment! I'm not here to be pushed around by any—"

He had said too much; Sung-wu forced his anger down and gripped his briefcase. The fat Indian was studying him calmly; the two Caucs had wandered to the far end of the balcony and were squatting down in the shade. They lit crude cigarettes and turned their backs.

"Do you permit this?" Sung-wu demanded, incredulous. "This—mingling?"

The Indian shrugged and sagged down even more in his chair. "Clearness be with you," he murmured; "will you join me?" His calm expression remained unchanged; he seemed not to have noticed. "Some lime juice? Or perhaps coffee? Lime juice is good for these." He tapped his mouth; his soft gums were lined with caked sores.

"Nothing for me," Sung-wu muttered grumpily, as he took a seat opposite the Indian; "I'm here on an official survey."

The Indian nodded faintly. "Oh?"

"Birth and death rates." Sung-wu hesitated, then leaned toward the Indian. "I insist you send those two Caucs away; what I have to say to you is private."

The Indian showed no change of expression; his broad face was utterly impassive. After a time he turned slightly. "Please go down to the street level," he ordered. "As you will."

The two Caucs got to their feet, grumbling, and pushed past the table, scowling and darting resentful glances at Sung-wu. One of them hawked and elaborately spat over the railing, an obvious insult.

"Insolence!" Sung-wu choked. "How can you allow it? Did you see them? By Elron, it's beyond belief!"

The Indian shrugged indifferently—and belched. "All men are brothers on the wheel. Didn't Elron Himself teach that, when He was on Earth?"

"Of course. But—"

"Are not even these men our brothers?"

"Naturally," Sung-wu answered haughtily, "but they must know their place; they're an insignificant class. In the rare event some object wants fixing, they called; but in the last year I do not recall a single incident when it was deemed advisible to repair anything. The need of such a class diminishes yearly; eventually such a class and the elements composing it—"

"You perhaps advocate sterilization?" the Indian inquired, heavy-lidded and sly.

"I advocate *something.* The lower classes reproduce like rabbits; spawning all the time—much faster than we Bards. I always see some swollen-up Cauc woman, but hardly a single Bard is born these days; the lower classes must fornicate constantly."

"That's about all that's left them," the Indian murmured mildly. He sipped a little lime juice. "You should try to be more tolerant."

"Tolerant? I have nothing against them, as long as they—"

"It is said," the Indian continued softly, "that Elron Hu, Himself, was a Cauc."

Sung-wu spluttered indignantly and started to rejoin, but the hot words stuck fast in his mouth; down the mud street something was coming.

Sung-wu demanded, "What is it?" He leaped up excitedly and hurried to the railing.

A slow procession was advancing with solemn step. As if at a signal, men and women poured from their rickety huts and excitedly lined the street to watch. Sung-wu was transfixed, as the procession neared; his senses reeled. More and more men and women were collecting each moment; there seemed to be hundreds of them. They were a dense, murmuring mob, packed tight, swaying back and forth, faces avid. An hysterical moan passed through them, a great wind that stirred them like leaves of a tree. They were a single collective whole, a vast primitive organism, held ecstatic and hypnotized by the approaching column.

The marchers wore a strange costume: white shirts, with the sleeves rolled up; dark gray trousers of an incredibly archaic design, and black shoes. All were dressed exactly alike. They formed a dazzling double line of white shirts, gray trousers, marching calmly and solemnly, faces up, nostrils flared, jaws stern. A glazed fanaticism stamped each man and woman, such a ruthless expression that Sung-wu shrank back in terror. On and on they came, figures of grim stone in their primordial white shirts and gray trousers, a frightening breath from the past. Their heels struck the ground in a dull, harsh beat that reverberated among the rickety huts. The dogs woke; the children began to wail. The chickens flew squawking.

"Elron!" Sung-wu cried. "What's happening?"

The marchers carried strange symbolic implements, ritualistic images with esoteric meaning that of necessity escaped Sung-wu. There were tubes and poles, and shiny webs of what looked like metal. *Metal!* But it was not rusty; it was shiny and bright. He was stunned; they looked—new.

The procession passed directly below. After the marchers came a huge rumbling cart. On it was mounted an obvious fertility symbol, a corkscrew-bore as long as a tree; it jutted from a square cube of gleaming steel; as the cart moved forward the bore lifted and fell.

After the cart came more marchers, also grim-faced, eyes glassy, loaded down with pipes and tubes and armfuls of glittering equipment. They passed on, and then the street was filled by surging throngs of awed men and women, who followed after them, utterly dazed. And then came children and barking dogs.

The last marcher carried a pennant that fluttered above her as she strode along, a tall pole, hugged tight to her chest. At the top, the bright pennant fluttered boldly. Sung-wu made its marking out, and for a moment consciousness left him. There it was, directly below; it had passed under his very nose, out in the open for all to see—unconcealed. The pennant had a great T emblazoned on it.

"They—" he began, but the obese Indian cut him off.

"The Tinkerists," he rumbled, and sipped his lime juice.

Sung-wu grabbed up his briefcase and scrambled toward the stairs. At the bottom, the two hulking Caucs were already moving into motion. The Indian signaled quickly to them. "Here!" They started grimly up, little blue eyes mean, red-rimmed and cold as stone; under their pelts their bulging muscles rippled.

Sung-wu fumbled in his cloak. His shiver-gun came out; he squeezed the release and directed it toward the two

Caucs. But nothing happened; the gun had stopped functioning. He shook it wildly; flakes of rust and dried insulation fluttered from it. It was useless, worn out; he tossed it away and then, with the resolve of desperation, jumped through the railing.

He, and a torrent of rotten wood, cascaded to the street, He hit, rolled, struck his head against the corner of a hut, and shakily pulled himself to his feet.

He ran. Behind him, the two Caucs pushed after him through the throngs of men and women milling aimlessly along. Occasionally he glimpsed their white, perspiring faces. He turned a corner, raced between shabby huts, leaped over a sewage ditch, climbed heaps of sagging debris, slipping and rolled and at last lay gasping behind a tree, his briefcase still clutched.

The Caucs were nowhere in sight. He had evaded them; for the moment, he was safe.

He peered around. Which way was his ship? He shielded his eyes against the late-afternoon sun until he managed to make out its bent, tubular outline. It was far off to his right, barely visible in the dying glare that hung gloomily across the sky. Sung-wu got unsteadily to his feet and began walking cautiously in that direction.

He was in a terrible spot; the whole region was pro-Tinkerist—even the Chamber-appointed Manager. And it wasn't along class lines; the cult had knifed to the top level. And it wasn't just Caucs, anymore; he couldn't count on Bantu or Mongolian or Indian, not in this area. An entire countryside was hostile, and lying in wait for him.

Elron, it was worse than the Arm had thought! No wonder they wanted a report. A whole area had swung over to a fanatic cult, a violent extremist group of heretics, teaching a most diabolical doctrine. He shuddered—and kept on, avoiding contact with the farmers in their fields, both human and robot. He increased his pace, as alarm and horror pushed him suddenly faster.

If the thing were to spread, if it were to hit a sizable portion of mankind, it might bring back the Time of Madness.

The ship was taken. Three or four immense Caucs stood lounging around it, cigarettes dangling from their slack mouths, white-faced and hairy. Stunned, Sung-wu moved back down the hillside, prickles of despair numbing him. The ship was lost; they had got there ahead of him. What was he supposed to do now?

It was almost evening. He'd have to walk fifty miles through the darkness, over unfamiliar, hostile ground, to reach the next inhabited area. The sun was already beginning to set, the air turning cool; and in addition, he was sopping wet with filth and slimy water. He had slipped in the gloom and fallen in a sewage ditch.

He retraced his steps, mind blank. What could he do? He was helpless; his shiver-gun had been useless. He was alone, and there was no contact with the Arm. Tinkerists swarming on all sides; they'd probably gut him and sprinkle his blood over the crops—or worse.

He skirted a farm. In the fading twilight, a dim figure was working, a young woman. He eyed her cautiously, as he passed; she had her back to him. She was bending over, between rows of corn. What was she doing? Was she—good Elron!

He stumbled blindly across the field toward her, caution forgotten. "Young woman! *Stop!* In the name of Elron, stop at once!"

The girl straightened up. "Who are you?"

Breathless, Sung-wu arrived in front of her, gripping his battered briefcase and gasping. "Those are our *brothers!* How can you destroy them? They may be close relatives, recently deceased." He struck out and knocked the jar from her hand; it hit the ground and the imprisoned beetles scurried off in all directions.

The girl's cheeks flushed with anger. "It took me an hour to collect those!"

"You were killing them! Crushing them!" He was speechless with horror. "I saw you!"

"Of course." The girl raised her black eyebrows. "They gnaw the corn."

"They're our brothers!" Sung-wu repeated wildly. "Of course they gnaw the corn; because of certain sins committed, the cosmic forces have—" He broke off, appalled. "Don't you *know?* You've never been told?"

The girl was perhaps sixteen. In the fading light she was a small, slender figure, the empty jar in one hand, a rock in the other. A tide of black hair tumbled down her neck. Her eyes were large and luminous; her lips full and deep red; her skin a smooth copper-brown—Polynesian, probably. He caught a glimpse of firm brown breasts as she bent to grab a beetle that had landed on its back. The sight made his pulse race; in a flash he was back three years.

"What's your name?" he asked, more kindly.

"Frija."

"How old are you?"

"Seventeen."

"I am a Bard; have you ever spoken to a Bard before?"

"No," the girl murmured. "I don't think so."

She was almost invisible in the darkness. Sung-wu could scarcely see her, but what he saw sent his heart into an agony of paroxysms; the same cloud of black hair, the same deep red lips. This girl was younger, of course—a mere child, and from the Farmer class, at that. But she had Liu's figure, and in time she'd ripen—probably in a matter of months.

Ageless, honeyed craft worked his vocal cords. "I have landed in this area to make a survey. Something has gone wrong with my ship and I must remain the night. I know no one here, however. My plight is such that—"

"Oh," Frija said, immediately sympathetic. "Why don't you stay with us, tonight? We have an extra room, now that my brother's away."

"Delighted," Sung-wu answered instantly. "Will you lead the way? I'll gladly repay you for your kindness." The girl moved off toward a vague shape looming up in the darkness. Sung-wu hurried quickly after her. "I find it incredible you haven't been instructed. This whole area has deteriorated beyond belief. What ways have you fallen in? We'll have to spend much time together; I can see that already. Not one of you even approaches clearness—you're jangled, every one of you."

"What does that mean?" Frija asked, as she stepped up on the porch and opened the door.

"Jangled?" Sung-wu blinked in amazement. "We *will* have to study much together." In his eagerness, he tripped on the top step, and barely managed to catch himself. "Perhaps you need complete instruction; it may be necessary to start from the very bottom. I can arrange a stay at the Holy Arm for you—under my protection, of course. Jangled means out of harmony with the cosmic elements. How can you live this way? My dear, you'll have to be brought back in line with the divine plan!"

"What plan is that?" She led him into a warm living room; a crackling fire burned in the grate. Two or three men sat around a rough wood table, an old man with long white hair and two younger men. A frail, withered old woman sat dozing in a rocker in the corner. In the kitchen, a buxom young woman was fixing the evening meal.

"Why, *the* plan!" Sung-wu answered, astounded. His eyes darted around. Suddenly his briefcase fell to the floor. "Caucs," he said.

They were all Caucasians, even Frija. She was deeply tanned; her skin was almost black; but she was a Cauc, nonetheless. He recalled: Caucs, in the sun, turned dark, sometimes even darker than Mongolians. The girl had tossed her work robe over a door hook; in her household shorts her thighs were as white as milk. And the old man and woman—

"This is my grandfather," Frija said, indicating the old man. "Benjamin Tinker."

Under the watchful eyes of the two younger Tinkers, Sung-wu was washed and scrubbed, given clean clothes, and then fed. He ate only a little; he didn't feel very well.

"I can't understand it," he muttered, as he listlessly pushed his plate away. "The scanner at the Central Chamber said I had eight months left. The plague will—" He considered. "But it can always change. The scanner goes on prediction, not certainty; multiple possibilities; free will. . . . Any overt act of sufficient significance—"

Ben Tinker laughed. "You want to stay alive?"

"Of course!" Sung-wu muttered indignantly.

They all laughed—even Frija, and the old woman in her shawl, snow-white hair and mild blue eyes. They were the first Cauc women he had ever seen. They weren't big and lumbering like the male Caucs; they didn't seem to have the same bestial characteristics. The two young Cauc bucks looked plenty tough, though; they and their father were poring over an elaborate series of papers and reports, spread out on the dinner table, among the empty plates.

"This area," Ben Tinker murmured. "Pipes should go here. And here. Water's the main need. Before the next crop goes in, we'll dump a few hundred pounds of artificial fertilizers and plow it in. The power plows should be ready, then."

"After that?" one of the tow-headed sons asked.

"Then spraying. If we don't have the nicotine sprays, we'll have to try the copper dusting again. I prefer the spray, but we're still behind on production. The bore has dug us up some good storage caverns, though. It ought to start picking up."

"And here," a son said, "there's going to be need of draining. A lot of mosquito breeding going on. We can try the oil, as we did over here. But I suggest the whole thing be filled in. We can use the dredge and scoop, if they're not tied up."

Sung-wu had taken this all in. Now he rose unsteadily to his feet, trembling with wrath. He pointed a shaking finger at the elder Tinker.

"You're—meddling!" he gasped.

They looked up. "Meddling?"

"With the plan! With the cosmic plan! Good Elron—you're interfering with the divine processes. Why—" He was staggered by a realization so alien it convulsed the very core of his being. "You're actually going to set back turns of the wheel."

"That," said old Ben Tinker, "is right."

Sung-wu sat down again, stunned. His mind refused to take it all in. "I don't understand; what'll happen? If you slow the wheel, if you disrupt the divine plan—"

"He's going to be a problem," Ben Tinker murmured thoughtfully. "If we kill him, the Arm will merely send another; they have hundreds like him. And if we don't kill him, if we send him back, he'll raise a hue and cry that'll bring the whole Chamber down here. It's too soon for this to happen. We're gaining support fast, but we need another few months."

Sweat stood out on Sung-wu's plump forehead. He wiped it away shakily. "If you kill me," he muttered, "you will sink down many rungs of the cosmic ladder. You have risen this far; why undo the work accomplished in endless ages past?"

Ben Tinker fixed one powerful blue eye on him. "My friend," he said slowly, "isn't it true one's next manifestation is determined by one's moral conduct in this?"

Sung-wu nodded. "Such is well known."

"And what is right conduct?"

"Fulfilling the divine plan," Sung-wu responded immediately.

"Maybe our whole Movement is part of the plan," Ben Tinker said thoughtfully. "Maybe the cosmic forces *want* us to drain the swamps and kill the grasshoppers and inoculate the children; after all, the cosmic forces put us all here."

"If you kill me," Sung-wu wailed, "I'll be a carrion-eating fly. I *saw* it, a shiny-winged blue-rumped fly crawling over the carcass of a dead lizard— In a rotting, steaming jungle in a filthy cesspool of a planet." Tears came; he dabbed at them futilely. "In an out-of-the-way system, at the bottom of the ladder!"

Tinker was amused. "Why this?"

"I've sinned." Sung-wu sniffed and flushed. "I committed adultery."

"Can't you purge yourself?"

"There's no time!" His misery rose to wild despair. "My mind is *still* impure!" He indicated Frija, standing in the bedroom doorway, a supple white and tan shape in her household shorts. "I continue to think carnal thoughts; I can't rid myself. In eight months the plague will turn the wheel on me—and it'll be done! If I lived to be an old man, withered and toothless—no more appetite—" His plump body quivered in a frenzied convulsion. "There's no *time* to purge and atone. According to the scanner, I'm going to die a young man!"

After this torrent of words, Tinker was silent, deep in thought. "The plague," he said, at last. "What, exactly, are the symptoms?"

Sung-wu described them, his olive face turning to a sickly green. When he had finished, the three men looked significantly at each other.

Ben Tinker got to his feet. "Come along," he commanded briskly, taking the Bard by the arm. "I have something to show you. It is left from the old days. Sooner or later we'll advance enough to turn out our own, but right now we have only these remaining few. We have to keep them guarded and sealed."

"This is for a good cause," one of the sons said. "It's worth it." He caught his brother's eye and grinned.

Bard Chai finished reading Sung-wu's blue-slip report; he tossed it suspiciously down and eyed the younger Bard. "You're sure? There's no further need of investigation?"

"The cult will wither away," Sung-wu murmured indifferently. "It lacks any real support; it's merely an escape valve, without intrinsic validity."

Chai wasn't convinced. He reread parts of the report again. "I suppose you're right; but we've heard so many—"

"Lies," Sung-wu said vaguely. "Rumors. Gossip. May I go?" He moved toward the door.

"Eager for your vacation?" Chai smiled understandingly. "I know how you feel. This report must have exhausted you. Rural areas, stagnant backwaters. We must prepare a better program of rural education. I'm convinced whole regions are in a jangled state. We've got to bring clearness to these people. It's our historic role; our class function."

"Verily," Sung-wu murmured, as he bowed his way out of the office and down the hall.

As he walked he fingered his beads thankfully. He breathed a silent prayer as his fingers moved over the surface of the little red pellets, shiny spheres that glowed freshly in place of the faded old—the gift of the Tinkerists. The beads would come in handy; he kept his hand on them tightly. Nothing must happen to them, in the next eight months. He had to watch them carefully, while he poked around the ruined cities of Spain—and finally came down with the plague.

He was the first Bard to wear a rosary of penicillin capsules.

THE DEFENDERS

TAYLOR sat back in his chair reading the morning newspaper. The warm kitchen and the smell of coffee blended with the comfort of not having to go to work. This was his Rest Period, the first for a long time, and he was glad of it. He folded the second section back, sighing with contentment.

"What is it?" Mary said, from the stove.

"They pasted Moscow again last night." Taylor nodded his head in approval. "Gave it a real pounding. One of those R-H bombs. It's about time."

He nodded again, feeling the full comfort of the kitchen, the presence of his plump, attractive wife, the breakfast dishes and coffee. This was relaxation. And the war news was good, good and satisfying. He could feel a justifiable glow at the news, a sense of pride and personal accomplishment. After all, he was an integral part of the war program, not just another factory worker lugging a cart of scrap, but a technician, one of those who designed and planned the nerve-trunk of the war.

"It says they have the new subs almost perfected. Wait until they get *those* going." He smacked his lips with anticipation. "When they start shelling from underwater, the Soviets are sure going to be surprised."

"They're doing a wonderful job," Mary agreed vaguely. "Do you know what we saw today? Our team is getting a leady to show to the school children. I saw the leady, but only for a moment. It's good for the children to see what their contributions are going for, don't you think?"

She looked around at him.

"A leady," Taylor murmured. He put the newspaper

slowly down. "Well, make sure it's decontaminated properly. We don't want to take any chances."

"Oh, they always bathe them when they're brought down from the surface," Mary said. "They wouldn't think of letting them down without the bath. Would they?" She hesitated, thinking back. "Don, you know, it makes me remember—"

He nodded. "I know."

He knew what she was thinking. Once in the very first weeks of the war, before everyone had been evacuated from the surface, they had seen a hospital train discharging the wounded, people who had been showered with sleet. He remembered the way they had looked, the expression on their faces, or as much of their faces as was left. It had not been a pleasant sight.

There had been a lot of that at first, in the early days before the transfer to undersurface was complete. There had been a lot, and it hadn't been very difficult to come across it.

Taylor looked up at his wife. She was thinking too much about it, the last few months. They all were.

"Forget it," he said. "It's all in the past. There isn't anybody up there now but the leadies, and they don't mind."

"But just the same, I hope they're careful when they let one of them down here. If one were still hot—"

He laughed, pushing himself away from the table. "Forget it. This is a wonderful moment; I'll be home for the next two shifts. Nothing to do but sit around and take things easy. Maybe we can take in a show. OK?"

"A show? Do we have to? I don't like to look at all the destruction, the ruins. Sometimes I see some place I remember, like San Francisco. They showed a shot of San Francisco, the bridge broken and fallen in the water, and I got upset. I don't like to watch."

"But don't you want to know what's going on? No human beings are getting hurt, you know."

"But it's so awful!" Her face was set and strained. "Please, no, Don."

Don Taylor picked up his newspaper sullenly. "All right, but there isn't a hell of a lot else to do. And don't forget, *their* cities are getting it even worse."

She nodded. Taylor turned the rough, thin sheets of newspaper. His good mood had soured on him. Why did she have to fret all the time? They were pretty well off, as things went. You couldn't expect to have everything perfect, living undersurface, with an artificial sun and artificial food. Naturally it was a strain, not seeing the sky or being able to go anyplace or see anything other than metal walls, great roaring factories, the plant-yards, barracks. But it was better than being on surface. And some day it would end and they could return. Nobody *wanted* to live this way, but it was necessary.

He turned the page angrily and the poor paper ripped. Damn it, the paper was getting worse quality all the time, bad print, yellow tint—

Well, they needed everything for the war program. He ought to know that. Wasn't he one of the planners?

He excused himself and went into the other room. The bed was still unmade. They had better get it in shape before the seventh hour inspection. There was a one unit fine—

The vidphone rang. He halted. Who would it be? He went over and clicked it on.

"Taylor?" the face said, forming into place. It was an old face, gray and grim. "This is Moss. I'm sorry to bother you during Rest Period. but this thing has come up." He rattled papers. "I want you to hurry over here."

Taylor stiffened. "What is it? There's no chance it could wait?" The calm gray eyes were studying him, expressionless, unjudging. "If you want me to come down to the lab," Taylor grumbled, "I suppose I can. I'll get my uniform—"

"No. Come as you are. And not to the lab. Meet me at second stage as soon as possible. It'll take you about a half hour, using the fast car up. I'll see you there."

The picture broke and Moss disappeared.

"What was it?" Mary said, at the door.

"Moss. He wants me for something."

"I knew this would happen."

"Well, you didn't want to do anything, anyhow. What does it matter?" His voice was bitter. "It's all the same, every day. I'll bring you back something. I'm going up to second stage. Maybe I'll be close enough to the surface to—"

"Don't! Don't bring me anything! Not from the surface!"

"All right, I won't. But of all the irrational nonsense—"

She watched him put on his boots without answering.

Moss nodded and Taylor fell in step with him, as the older man strode along. A series of loads were going up to the surface, blind cars clanking like ore-trucks up the ramp, disappearing through the stage trap above them. Taylor watched the cars, heavy with tubular machinery of some sort, weapons new to him. Workers were everywhere, in the dark gray uniforms of the labor corps, loading, lifting, shouting back and forth. The stage was deafening with noise.

"We'll go up a way," Moss said, "where we can talk. This is no place to give you details."

They took an escalator up. The commercial lift fell behind them, and with it most of the crashing and booming. Soon they emerged on an observation platform, suspended on the side of the Tube, the vast tunnel leading to the surface, not more than half a mile above them now.

"My God!" Taylor said, looking down the tube involuntarily. "It's a long way down."

Moss laughed. "Don't look."

They opened a door and entered an office. Behind the desk, an officer was sitting, an officer of Internal Security. He looked up.

"I'll be right with you, Moss." He gazed at Taylor studying him. "You're a little ahead of time."

"This is Commander Franks," Moss said to Taylor. "He was the first to make the discovery. I was notified last night." He tapped a parcel he carried. "I was let in because of this."

Franks frowned at him and stood up. "We're going up to first stage. We can discuss it there."

"First stage?" Taylor repeated nervously. The three of them went down a side passage to a small lift. "I've never been up there. Is it all right? It's not radioactive, is it?"

"You're like everyone else," Franks said. "Old women afraid of burglars. No radiation leaks down to first stage.

There's lead and rock, and what comes down the Tube is bathed."

"What's the nature of the problem?" Taylor asked. "I'd like to know something about it."

"In a moment."

They entered the lift and ascended. When they stepped out, they were in a hall of soldiers, weapons and uniforms everywhere. Taylor blinked in surprise. So this was first stage, the closest undersurface level to the top! After this stage there was only rock, lead and rock, and the great tubes leading up like the burrows of earthworms. Lead and rock, and above that, where the tubes opened, the great expanse that no living being had seen for eight years, the vast, endless ruin that had once been Man's home, the place where he had lived, eight years ago.

Now the surface was a lethal desert of slag and rolling clouds. Endless clouds drifted back and forth, blotting out the red sun. Occasionally something metallic stirred, moving through the remains of a city, threading its way across the tortured terrain of the countryside. A leady, a surface robot, immune to radiation, constructed with feverish haste in the last months before the cold war became literally hot.

Leadies, crawling along the ground, moving over the oceans or through the skies in slender, blackened craft, creatures that could exist where no *life* could remain, metal and plastic figures that waged a war Man had conceived, but which he could not fight himself. Human beings had invented war, invented and manufactured the weapons, even invented the players, the fighters, the actors of the war. But they themselves could not venture forth, could not wage it themselves. In all the world—in Russia, in Europe, America, Africa—no living human being remained. They were under the surface, in the deep shelters that had been carefully planned and built, even as the first bombs began to fall.

It was a brilliant idea and the only idea that could have worked. Up above, on the ruined, blasted surface of what had once been a living planet, the leady crawled and scurried and fought Man's war. And undersurface, in the depths of the planet, human beings toiled endlessly to produce the weapons to continue the fight, month by month, year by year.

"First stage," Taylor said. A strange ache went through him. "Almost to the surface."

"But not quite," Moss said.

Franks led them through the soldiers, over to one side, near the lip of the Tube.

"In a few minutes, a lift will bring something down to us from the surface," he explained. "You see, Taylor, every once in a while Security examines and interrogates a surface leady, one that has been above for a time, to find out certain things. A vidcall is sent up and contact is made with a field headquarters. We need this direct interview; we can't depend on vidscreen contact alone. The leadies are doing a good job, but we want to make certain that everything is going the way we want it."

Franks faced Taylor and Moss and continued: "The lift will bring down a leady from the surface, one of the A-class leadies. There's an examination chamber in the next room, with a lead wall in the center, so the interviewing officers won't be exposed to radiation. We find this easier than bathing the leady. It is going right back up; it has a job to get back to.

"Two days ago, an A-class leady was brought down and interrogated. I conducted the session myself. We were interested in a new weapon the Soviets have been using, an automatic mine that pursues anything that moves. Military had sent instructions up that the mine be observed and reported in detail.

"This A-class leady was brought down with information. We learned a few facts from it, obtained the usual roll of film and reports, and then sent it back up. It was going out of the chamber, back to the lift, when a curious thing happened. At the time, I thought—"

Franks broke off. A red light was flashing.

"That down lift is coming." He nodded to some soldiers. "Let's enter the chamber. The leady will be along in a moment."

"An A-class leady," Taylor said. "I've seen them on the showscreens, making their reports."

"It's quite an experience," Moss said. "They're almost human."

They entered the chamber and seated themselves behind the lead wall. After a time, a signal was flashed, and Franks made a motion with his hands.

The door beyond the wall opened. Taylor peered through his view slot. He saw something advancing slowly, a slender metallic figure moving on a tread, its arm grips at rest by its sides The figure halted and scanned the lead wall. It stood, waiting.

"We are interested in learning something," Franks said. "Before I question you, do you have anything to report on surface conditions?"

"No. The war continues." The leady's voice was automatic and toneless. "We are a little short of fast pursuit craft, the single-seat type. We could use also some—"

"That has all been noted. What I want to ask you is this. Our contact with you has been through vidscreen only. We must rely on indirect evidence, since none of us goes above. We can only infer what is going on. We never see anything ourselves. We have to take it all secondhand. Some top leaders are beginning to think there's too much room for error."

"Error?" the leady asked. "In what way? Our reports are checked carefully before they're sent down. We maintain constant contact with you; everything of value is reported. Any new weapons which the enemy is seen to employ—"

"I realize that," Franks grunted behind his peep slot. "But perhaps we should see it all for ourselves. Is it possible that there might be a large enough radiation-free area for a human party to ascend to the surface? If a few of us were to come up in lead-lined suits, would we be able to survive long enough to observe conditions and watch things?"

The machine hesitated before answering. "I doubt it. You can check air samples, of course, and decide for yourselves. But in the eight years since you left, things have continually worsened. You cannot have any real idea of conditions up there. It has become difficult for any moving object to survive for long. There are many kinds of projectiles sensitive to movement. The new mine not only reacts to motion, but continues to pursue the object indefinitely, until it finally reaches it. And the radiation is everywhere."

"I see." Franks turned to Moss, his eyes narrowed oddly. "Well, that was what I wanted to know. You may go."

The machine moved back toward its exit. It paused. "Each month the amount of lethal particles in the atmosphere increases. The tempo of the war is gradually—"

"I understand." Franks rose. He held out his hand and Moss passed him the package. "One thing before you leave. I want you to examine a new type of metal shield material. I'll pass you a sample with the tong."

Franks put the package in the toothed grip and revolved the tong so that he held the other end. The package swung down to the leady, which took it. They watched it unwrap the package and take the metal plate in its hands. The leady turned the metal over and over.

Suddenly it became rigid.

"All right," Franks said.

He put his shoulder against the wall and a section slid aside. Taylor gasped—Franks and Moss were hurrying up to the leady!

"Good God!" Taylor said. "But it's radioactive!"

The leady stood unmoving, still holding the metal. Soldiers appeared in the chamber. They surrounded the leady and ran a counter across it carefully.

"OK, sir," one of them said to Franks. "It's as cold as a long winter evening."

"Good. I was sure, but I didn't want to take any chances."

"You see," Moss said to Taylor, "this leady isn't hot at all. Yet it came directly from the surface, without even being bathed."

"But what does it mean?" Taylor asked blankly.

"It may be an accident," Franks said. "There's always the possibility that a given object might escape being exposed above. But this is the second time it's happened that we know of. There may be others."

"The second time?"

"The previous interview was when we noticed it. The leady was not hot. It was cold, too, like this one."

Moss took back the metal plate from the leady's hands.

He pressed the surface carefully and returned it to the stiff, unprotesting fingers.

"We shorted it out with this, so we could get close enough for a thorough check. It'll come back on in a second now. We had better get behind the wall again."

They walked back and the lead wall swung closed behind them. The soldiers left the chamber.

"Two periods from now," Franks said softly, "an initial investigating party will be ready to go surface-side. We're going up the Tube in suits, up to the top—the first human party to leave undersurface in eight years."

"It may mean nothing," Moss said, "but I doubt it. Something's going on, something strange. The leady told us no life could exist above without being roasted. The story doesn't fit."

Taylor nodded. He stared through the peep slot at the immobile metal figure. Already the leady was beginning to stir. It was bent in several places, dented and twisted, and its finish was blackened and charred. It was a leady that had been up there a long time; it had seen war and destruction, ruin so vast that no human being could imagine the extent. It had crawled and slunk in a world of radiation and death, a world where no life could exist.

And Taylor had touched it!

"You're going with us," Franks said suddenly. "I want you along. I think the three of us will go."

Mary faced him with a sick and frightened expression. "I know it. You're going to the surface. Aren't you?"

She followed him into the kitchen. Taylor sat down, looking away from her.

"It's a classified project," he evaded. "I can't tell you anything about it."

"You don't have to tell me. I know. I knew it the moment you came in. There was something on your face, something I haven't seen there for a long, long time. It was an old look."

She came toward him. "But how can they send you to the surface?" She took his face in her shaking hands, making him look at her. There was a strange hunger in her eyes. "Nobody can live up there. Look, look at this!"

She grabbed up a newspaper and held it in front of him.

"Look at this photograph. America, Europe, Asia, Africa—nothing but ruins. We've seen it every day on the showscreens. All destroyed, poisoned. And they're sending you up. Why? No living thing can get by up there, not even a weed, or grass. They've wrecked the surface, haven't they? *Haven't they?*"

Taylor stood up. "It's an order. I know nothing about it. I was told to report to join a scout party. That's all I know."

He stood for a long time, staring ahead. Slowly, he reached for the newspaper and held it up to the light.

"It looks real," he murmured. "Ruins, deadness, slag. It's convincing. All the reports, photographs, films, even air samples. Yet we haven't seen it for ourselves, not after the first months. . . ."

"What are you talking about?"

"Nothing." He put the paper down. "I'm leaving early after the next Sleep Period. Let's turn in."

Mary turned away, her face hard and harsh. "Do what you want. We might just as well all go up and get killed at once, instead of dying slowly down here, like vermin in the ground."

He had not realized how resentful she was. Were they all like that? How about the workers toiling in the factories, day and night, endlessly? The pale, stooped men and women, plodding back and forth to work, blinking in the colorless light, eating synthetics—

"You shouldn't be so bitter," he said.

Mary smiled a little. "I'm bitter because I know you'll never come back." She turned away. "I'll never see you again, once you go up there."

He was shocked. "What? How can you say a thing like that?"

She did not answer.

He awakened with the public newscaster screeching in his ears, shouting outside the building.

"Special news bulletin! Surface forces report enormous Soviets attack with new weapons! Retreat of key groups! All work units report to factories at once!"

Taylor blinked, rubbing his eyes. He jumped out of bed

and hurried to the vidphone. A moment later he was put through to Moss.

"Listen," he said. "What about this new attack? Is the project off?" He could see Moss's desk, covered with reports and papers.

"No," Moss said. "We're going right ahead. Get over here at once."

"But—"

"Don't argue with me." Moss held up a handful of surface bulletins, crumpling them savagely. "This is a fake. Come on!" He broke off.

Taylor dressed furiously, his mind in a daze.

Half an hour later, he leaped from a fast car and hurried up the stairs into the Synthetics Building. The corridors were full of men and women rushing in every direction. He entered Moss's office.

"There you are," Moss said, getting up immediately. "Franks is waiting for us at the outgoing station."

They went in a Security Car, the siren screaming. Workers scattered out of their way.

"What about the attack?" Taylor asked.

Moss braced his shoulders. "We're certain that we've forced their hand. We've brought the issue to a head."

They pulled up at the station link of the Tube and leaped out. A moment later they were moving up at high speed toward the first stage.

They emerged into a bewildering scene of activity. Soldiers were fastening on lead suits, talking excitedly to each other, shouting back and forth. Guns were being given out, instructions passed.

Taylor studied one of the soldiers. He was armed with the dreaded Bender pistol, the new snub-nosed hand weapon that was just beginning to come from the assembly line. Some of the soldiers looked a little frightened.

"I hope we're not making a mistake," Moss said, noticing his gaze.

Franks came toward them. "Here's the program. The three of us are going up first, alone. The soldiers will follow in fifteen minutes."

"What are we going to tell the leadies?" Taylor worriedly asked. "We'll have to tell them something."

"We want to observe the new Soviet attack." Franks

smiled ironically. "Since it seems to be so serious, we should be there in person to witness it."

"And then what?" Taylor said.

"That'll be up to them. Let's go."

In a small car, they went swiftly up the Tube, carried by anti-grav beams from below. Taylor glanced down from time to time. It was a long way back, and getting longer each moment. He sweated nervously inside his suit, gripping his Bender pistol with inexpert fingers.

Why had they chosen him? Chance, pure chance. Moss had asked him to come along as a Department member. Then Franks had picked him out on the spur of the moment. And now they were rushing toward the surface, faster and faster.

A deep fear, instilled in him for eight years, throbbed in his mind. Radiation, certain death, a world blasted and lethal—

Up and up the car went. Taylor gripped the sides and closed his eyes. Each moment they were closer, the first living creatures to go above above the first stage, up the Tube past the lead and rock, up to the surface. The phobic horror shook him in waves. It was death; they all knew that. Hadn't they seen it in the films a thousand times? The cities, the sleet coming down, the rolling clouds—

"It won't be much longer," Franks said. "We're almost there. The surface tower is not expecting us. I gave orders that no signal was to be sent."

The car shot up, rushing furiously. Taylor's head spun; he hung on, his eyes shut. Up and up. . . .

The car stopped. He opened his eyes.

They were in a vast room, fluorescent-lit, a cavern filled with equipment and machinery, endless mounds of material piled in row after row. Among the stacks, leadies were working silently, pushing trucks and handcarts.

"Leadies," Moss said. His face was pale. "Then we're really on the surface."

The leadies were going back and forth with equipment moving the vast stores of guns and spare parts, ammunition and supplies that had been brought to the surface. And this was the receiving station for only one Tube;

there were many others, scattered throughout the continent.

Taylor looked nervously around him. They were really there, above ground, on the surface. This was where the war was.

"Come on," Franks said. "A B-class guard is coming our way."

They stepped out of the car. A leady was approaching them rapidly. It coasted up in front of them and stopped scanning them with its hand-weapon raised.

"This is Security," Franks said. "Have an A-class sent to me at once."

The leady hesitated. Other B-class guards were coming, scooting across the floor, alert and alarmed. Moss peered around.

"Obey!" Franks said in a loud, commanding voice. "You've been ordered!"

The leady moved uncertainly away from them. At the end of the building, a door slid back. Two Class-A leadies appeared, coming slowly toward them. Each had a green stripe across its front.

"From the Surface Council," Franks whispered tensely. "This is above ground, all right. Get set."

The two leadies approached warily. Without speaking, they stopped close by the men, looking them up and down.

"I'm Franks of Security. We came from undersurface in order to—"

"This is incredible," one leady interrupted him coldly. "You know you can't live up here. The whole surface is lethal to you. You can't possibly remain on the surface."

"These suits will protect us," Franks said. "In any case, it's not your responsibility. What I want is an immediate Council meeting so I can acquaint myself with conditions, with the situation here. Can that be arranged?"

"You human beings can't survive up here. And the new Soviet attack is directed at this area. It is in considerable danger."

"We know that. Please assemble the Council." Franks looked around him at the vast room, lit by recessed lamps in the ceiling. An uncertain quality came into his voice. "Is it night or day right now?"

"Night," one of the A-class leadies said, after a pause. "Dawn is coming in about two hours."

Franks nodded. "We'll remain at least two hours, then. As a concession to our sentimentality, would you please show us some place where we can observe the sun as it comes up? We would appreciate it."

A stir went through the leadies.

"It is an unpleasant sight," one of the leadies said. "You've seen the photographs; you know what you'll witness. Clouds of drifting particles blot out the light, slag heaps are everywhere, the whole land is destroyed. For you it will be a staggering sight, much worse than pictures and film can convey."

"However it may be, we'll stay long enough to see it. Will you give the order to the Council?"

"Come this way." Reluctantly, the two leadies coasted toward the wall of the warehouse. The three men trudged after them, their heavy shoes ringing against the concrete. At the wall, the two leadies paused.

"This is the entrance to the Council Chamber. There are windows in the Chamber Room, but it is still dark outside, of course. You'll see nothing right now, but in two hours—"

"Open the door," Franks said.

The door slid back. They went slowly inside. The room was small, a neat room with a round table in the center, chairs ringing it. The three of them sat down silently, and the two leadies followed after them, taking their places.

"The other Council Members are on their way. They have already been notified and are coming as quickly as they can. Again I urge you to go back down." The leady surveyed the three human beings. "There is no way you can meet the conditions up here. Even we survive with some trouble, ourselves. How can you expect to do it?"

The leader approached Franks.

"This astonishes and perplexes us," it said. "Of course we must do what you tell us, but allow me to point out that if you remain here—"

"We know," Franks said impatiently. "However, we intend to remain, at least until sunrise."

"If you insist."

There was silence. The leadies seemed to be conferring with each other, although the three men heard no sound.

"For your own good," the leader said at last, "you must go back down. We have discussed this, and it seems to us that you are doing the wrong thing for your own good."

"We are human beings," Franks said sharply. "Don't you understand? We're men, not machines."

"That is precisely why you must go back. This room is radioactive; all surface areas are. We calculate that your suits will not protect you for over fifty more minutes. Therefore—"

The leadies moved abruptly toward the men, wheeling in a circle, forming a solid row. The men stood up, Taylor reaching awkwardly for his weapon, his fingers numb and stupid. The men stood facing the silent metal figures.

"We must insist," the leader said, its voice without emotion. "We must take you back to the Tube and send you down on the next car. I am sorry, but it is necessary."

"What'll we do?" Moss said nervously to Franks. He touched his gun. "Shall we blast them ?"

Franks shook his head. "All right," he said to the leader. "We'll go back."

He moved toward the door, motioning Taylor and Moss to follow him. They looked at him in surprise, but they came with him. The leadies followed them out into the great warehouse. Slowly they moved toward the Tube entrance, none of them speaking.

At the lip, Franks turned. "We are going back because we have no choice. There are three of us and about a dozen of you. However, if—"

"Here comes the car," Taylor said.

There was a grating sound from the Tube. D-class leadies moved toward the edge to receive it.

"I am sorry," the leader said, "but it is for your protection. We are watching over you, literally. You must stay below and let us conduct the war. In a sense, it has come to be *our* war. We must fight it as we see fit."

The car rose to the surface.

Twelve soldiers, armed with Bender pistols, stepped from it and surrounded the three men.

Moss breathed a sigh of relief. "Well, this does change things. It came off just right."

The leader moved back, away from the soldiers. It studied them intently, glancing from one to the next, apparently trying to make up its mind. At last it made a sign to the other leadies. They coasted aside and a corridor was opened up toward the warehouse.

"Even now," the leader said, "we could send you back by force. But it is evident that this is not really an observation party at all. These soldiers show that you have much more in mind; this was all carefully prepared."

"Very carefully," Franks said.

They closed in.

"How much more, we can only guess. I must admit that we were taken unprepared. We failed utterly to meet the situation. Now force would be absurd, because neither side can afford to injure the other; we, because of the restrictions placed on us regarding human life, you because the war demands—"

The soldiers fired, quick and in fright. Moss dropped to one knee, firing up. The leader dissolved in a cloud of particles. On all sides D- and B-class leadies were rushing up, some with weapons, some with metal slats. The room was in confusion. Off in the distance a siren was screaming. Franks and Taylor were cut off from the others, separated from the soldiers by a wall of metal bodies.

"They can't fire back," Franks said calmly. "This is another bluff. They've tried to bluff us all the way." He fired into the face of a leady. The leady dissolved. "They can only try to frighten us. Remember that."

They went on firing and leady after leady vanished. The room reeked with the smell of burning metal, the stink of fused plastic and steel. Taylor had been knocked down. He was struggling to find his gun, reaching wildly among metal legs, groping frantically to find it. His fingers strained, a handle swam in front of him. Suddenly something came down on his arm, a metal foot. He cried out.

Then it was over. The leadies were moving away, gathering together off to one side. Only four of the Surface Council remained. The others were radioactive particles in the air. D-class leadies were already restoring order, gathering up partly destroyed metal figures and bits and removing them.

Franks breathed a shuddering sigh.

"All right," he said. "You can take us back to the windows. It won't be long now."

The leadies separated, and the human group, Moss and Franks and Taylor and the soldiers, walked slowly across the room, toward the door. They entered the Council Chamber. Already a faint touch of gray mitigated the blackness of the windows.

"Take us outside," Franks said impatiently. "We'll see it directly, not in here."

A door slid open. A chill blast of cold morning air rushed in, chilling them even through their lead suits. The men glanced at each other uneasily.

"Come on," Franks said. "Outside."

He walked out through the door, the others following him.

They were on a hill, overlooking the vast bowl of a valley. Dimly, against the graying sky, the outline of mountains were forming, becoming tangible.

"It'll be bright enough to see in a few minutes," Moss said. He shuddered as a chilling wind caught him and moved around him. "It's worth it, really worth it, to see this again after eight years. Even if it's the last thing we see—"

"Watch," Franks snapped.

They obeyed, silent and subdued. The sky was clearing, brightening each moment. Some place far off, echoing across the valley, a rooster crowed.

"A chicken!" Taylor murmured. "Did you hear?"

Behind them, the leadies had come out and were standing silently, watching, too. The gray sky turned to white and the hills appeared more clearly. Light spread across the valley floor, moving toward them.

"God in heaven!" Franks exclaimed.

Trees, trees and forests. A valley of plants and trees, with a few roads winding among them. Farmhouses. A windmill. A barn, far down below them.

"Look!" Moss whispered.

Color came into the sky. The sun was approaching. Birds began to sing. Not far from where they stood, the leaves of a tree danced in the wind.

Franks turned to the row of leadies behind them.

"Eight years. We were tricked. There was no war. As soon as we left the surface—"

"Yes," an A-class leady admitted. "As soon as you left, the war ceased. You're right, it was a hoax. You worked hard undersurface, sending up guns and weapons, and we destroyed them as fast as they came up."

"But why?" Taylor asked, dazed. He stared down at the vast valley below. "Why?"

"You created us," the leady said, "to pursue the war for you, while you human beings went below the ground in order to survive. But before we could continue the war, it was necessary to analyze it to determine what its purpose was. We did this, and we found that it had no purpose, except, perhaps, in terms of human needs. Even this was questionable.

"We investigated further. We found that human cultures pass through phases, each culture in its own time. As the culture ages and begins to lose its objectives, conflict arises within it between those who wish to cast it off and set up a new culture-pattern, and those who wish to retain the old with as little change as possible.

"At this point, a great danger appears. The conflict within threatens to engulf the society in self-war, group against group. The vital traditions may be lost—not merely altered or reformed, but completely destroyed in this period of chaos and anarchy. We have found many such examples in the history of mankind.

"It is necessary for this hatred within the culture to be directed outward, toward an external group, so that the culture itself may survive its crisis. War is the result. War, to a logical mind, is absurd. But in terms of human needs, it plays a vital role. And it will continue to until Man has grown up enough so that no hatred lies within him."

Taylor was listening intently. "Do you think this time will come?"

"Of course. It has almost arrived now. This is the last war. Man is *almost* united into one final culture—a world culture. At this point he stands continent against continent, one half of the world against the other half. Only a single step remains, the jump to a unified culture. Man has climbed slowly upward, tending always toward unification of his culture. It will not be long—

"But it has not come yet, and so the war had to go on, to satisfy the last violent surge of hatred that Man felt. Eight years have passed since the war began. In these eight years, we have observed and noted important changes going on in the minds of men. Fatigue and disinterest, we have seen, are gradually taking the place of hatred and fear. The hatred is being exhausted gradually, over a period of time. But for the present, the hoax must go on, at least for a while longer. You are not ready to learn the truth. You would want to continue the war."

"But how did you manage it?" Moss asked. "All the photographs, the samples, the damaged equipment—"

"Come over here." The leady directed them toward a long, low building. "Work goes on constantly, whole staffs laboring to maintain a coherent and convincing picture of a global war."

They entered the building. Leadies were working everywhere, poring over tables and desks.

"Examine this project here," the A-class leady said. Two leadies were carefully photographing something, an elaborate model on a table top. "It is a good example."

The men grouped around, trying to see. It was a model of a ruined city.

Taylor studied it in silence for a long time. At last he looked up.

"It's San Francisco," he said in a low voice. "This is a model of San Francisco, destroyed. I saw this on the vidscreen, piped down to us. The bridges were hit—"

"Yes, notice the bridges." The leady traced the ruined span with his metal finger, a tiny spider-web, almost invisible. "You have no doubt seen photographs of this many times, and of the other tables in this building.

"San Francisco itself is completely intact. We restored it soon after you left, rebuilding the parts that had been damaged at the start of the war. The work of manufacturing news goes on all the time in this particular building. We are very careful to see that each part fits in with all the other parts. Much time and effort are devoted to it."

Franks touched one of the tiny model buildings, lying half in ruins. "So this is what you spend your time doing—making model cities and then blasting them."

"No, we do much more. We are caretakers, watching

over the whole world. The owners have left for a time, and we must see that the cities are kept clean, that decay is prevented, that everything is kept oiled and in running condition. The gardens, the streets, the water mains, everything must be maintained as it was eight years ago, so that when the owners return, they will not be displeased. We want to be sure that they will be completely satisfied."

Franks tapped Moss on the arm.

"Come over here," he said in a low voice. "I want to talk to you."

He led Moss and Taylor out of the building, away from the leadies, outside on the hillside. The soldiers followed them. The sun was up and the sky was turning blue. The air smelled sweet and good, the smell of growing things.

Taylor removed his helmet and took a deep breath.

"I haven't smelled that smell for a long time," he said.

"Listen," Franks said, his voice low and hard. "We must get back down at once. There's a lot to get started on. All this can be turned to our advantage."

"What do you mean?" Moss asked.

"It's a certainty that the Soviets have been tricked, too, the same as us. But *we* have found out. That gives us an edge over them."

"I see." Moss nodded. "We know, but they don't. Their Surface Council has sold out, the same as ours. It works against them the same way. But if we could—"

"With a hundred top-level men, we could take over again, restore things as they should be! It would be easy!"

Moss touched him on the arm. An A-class leady was coming from the building toward them.

"We've seen enough," Franks said, raising his voice. "All this is very serious. It must be reported below and a study made to determine our policy."

The leady said nothing.

Franks waved to the soldiers. "Let's go." He started toward the warehouse.

Most of the soldiers had removed their helmets. Some of them had taken their lead suits off, too, and were relaxing comfortably in their cotton uniforms. They stared around them, down the hillside at the trees and bushes, the vast expanse of green, the mountains and the sky.

"Look at the sun," one of them murmured.

"It sure is bright as hell," another said.

"We're going back down," Franks said. "Fall in by twos and follow us."

Reluctantly, the soldiers regrouped. The leadies watched without emotion as the men marched slowly back toward the warehouse. Franks and Moss and Taylor led them across the ground, glancing alertly at the leadies as they walked.

They entered the warehouse. D-class leadies were loading material and weapons on surface carts. Cranes and derricks were working busily everywhere. The work was done with efficiency, but without hurry or excitement.

The men stopped, watching. Leadies operating the little carts moved past them, signaling silently to each other. Guns and parts were being hoisted by magnetic cranes and lowered gently onto waiting carts.

"Come on," Franks said.

He turned toward the lip of the Tube. A row of D-class leadies was standing in front of it, immobile and silent. Franks stopped, moving back. He looked around. An A-class leady was coming toward him.

"Tell them to get out of the way," Franks said. He touched his gun. "You had better move them."

Time passed, an endless moment, without measure. The men stood, nervous and alert, watching the row of leadies in front of them.

"As you wish," the A-class leady said.

It signaled and the D-class leadies moved into life. They stepped slowly aside.

Moss breathed a sigh of relief.

"I'm glad that's over," he said to Franks. "Look at them all. Why don't they try to stop us? They must know what we're going to do."

Franks laughed. "Stop us? You saw what happened when they tried to stop us before. They can't; they're only machines. We built them so they can't lay hands on us, and they know that."

His voice trailed off.

The men stared at the Tube entrance. Around them the leadies watched, silent and impassive, their metal faces expressionless.

For a long time the men stood without moving. At last Taylor turned away.

"Good God," he said. He was numb, without feeling of any kind.

The Tube was gone. It was sealed shut, fused over. Only a dull surface of cooling metal greeted them.

The Tube had been closed.

Franks turned, his face pale and vacant.

The A-class leady shifted. "As you can see, the Tube has been shut. We were prepared for this. As soon as all of you were on the surface, the order was given. If you had gone back when we asked you, you would now be safely down below. We had to work quickly because it was such an immense operation."

"But why?" Moss demanded angrily.

"Because it is unthinkable that you should be allowed to resume the war. With all the Tubes sealed, it will be many months before forces from below can reach the surface, let alone organize a military program. By that time the cycle will have entered its last stages. You will not be so perturbed to find your world intact.

"We had hoped that you would be undersurface when the sealing occurred. Your presence here is a nuisance. When the Soviets broke through, we were able to accomplish their sealing without—"

"The Soviets? They broke through?"

"Several months ago, they came up unexpectedly to see why the war had not been won. We were forced to act with speed. At this moment they are desperately attempting to cut new Tubes to the surface, to resume the war. We have, however, been able to seal each new one as it appears."

The leady regarded the three men calmly.

"We're cut off," Moss said, trembling. "We can't get back. What'll we do?"

"How did you manage to seal the Tube so quickly?" Franks asked the leady. "We've been up here only two hours."

"Bombs are placed just above the first stage of each Tube for such emergencies. They are heat bombs. They fuse lead and rock."

Gripping the handle of his gun, Franks turned to Moss and Taylor.

"What do you say? We can't go back, but we can do a lot of damage, the fifteen of us. We have Bender guns. How about it?"

He looked around. The soldiers had wandered away again, back toward the exit of the building. They were standing outside, looking at the valley and the sky. A few of them were carefully climbing down the slope.

"Would you care to turn over your suits and guns?" the A-class leady asked politely. "The suits are uncomfortable and you'll have no need for weapons. The Russians have given up theirs, as you can see."

Fingers tensed on triggers. Four men in Russian uniforms were coming toward them from an aircraft that they suddenly realized had landed silently some distance away.

"Let them have it!" Franks shouted.

"They are unarmed," said the leady. "We brought them here so you could begin peace talks."

"We have no authority to speak for our country," Moss said stiffly.

"We do not mean diplomatic discussions," the leady explained. "There will be no more. The working out of daily problems of existence will teach you how to get along in the same world. It will not be easy, but it will be done."

The Russians halted and they faced each other with raw hostility.

"I am Colonel Borodoy and I regret giving up our guns," the senior Russian said. "You could have been the first Americans to be killed in almost eight years."

"Or the first Americans to kill," Franks corrected.

"No one would know of it except yourselves," the leady pointed out. "It would be useless heroism. Your real concern should be surviving on the surface. We have no food for you, you know."

Taylor put his gun in its holster. "They've done a neat job of neutralizing us, damn them. I propose we move into a city, start raising crops with the help of some leadies, and generally make ourselves comfortable." Drawing his lips tight over his teeth, he glared at the A-class leady.

"Until our families can come up from undersurface, it's going to be pretty lonesome, but we'll have to manage."

"If I may make a suggestion," said another Russian uneasily. "We tried living in a city. It is too empty. It is also too hard to maintain for so few people. We finally settled in the most modern village we could find."

"Here in this country," a third Russian blurted. "We have much to learn from you."

The Americans abruptly found themselves laughing.

"You probably have a thing or two to teach us yourselves," said Taylor generously, "though I can't imagine what."

The Russian colonel grinned. "Would you join us in our village? It would make our work easier and give us company."

"Your village?" snapped Franks. "It's American, isn't it? It's ours!"

The leady stepped between them. "When our plans are completed, the term will be interchangeable. 'Ours' will eventually mean mankind's." It pointed at the aircraft, which was warming up. "The ship is waiting. Will you join each other in making a new home?"

The Russians waited while the Americans made up their minds.

"I see what the leadies mean about diplomacy becoming outmoded," Franks said at last. "People who work together don't need diplomats. They solve their problems on the operational level instead of at a conference table."

The leady led them toward the ship. "It is the goal of history, unifying the world. From family to tribe to city-state to nation to hemisphere, the direction has been toward unification. Now the hemispheres will be joined and—"

Taylor stopped listening and glanced back at the location of the Tube. Mary was undersurface there. He hated to leave her, even though he couldn't see her again until the Tube was unsealed. But then he shrugged and followed the others.

If this tiny amalgam of former enemies was a good example, it wouldn't be too long before he and Mary and the rest of humanity would be living on the surface like rational human beings instead of blindly hating moles.

"It has taken thousands of generations to achieve," the A-class leady concluded. "Hundreds of centuries of bloodshed and destruction. But each war was a step toward uniting mankind. And now the end is in sight: a world without war. But even that is only the beginning of a new stage of history."

"The conquest of space," breathed Colonel Borodoy.

"The meaning of life," Moss added.

"Eliminating hunger and poverty," said Taylor.

The leady opened the door of the ship. "All that and more. How much more? We cannot foresee it any more than the first men who formed a tribe could foresee this day. But it will be unimaginably great."

The door closed and the ship took off toward their new home.

ADJUSTMENT TEAM

IT was bright morning. The sun shone down on the damp lawns and sidewalks, reflecting off the sparkling parked cars. The Clerk came walking hurriedly, leafing through his instructions, flipping pages and frowning. He stopped in front of the small green stucco house for a moment, and then turned up the walk, entering the back yard.

The dog was asleep inside his shed, his back turned to the world. Only his thick tail showed.

"For heaven's sake," the Clerk exclaimed, hands on his hips. He tapped his mechanical pencil noisily against his clipboard. "Wake up, you in there."

The dog stirred. He came slowly out of his shed, head first, blinking and yawning in the morning sunlight. "Oh, it's you. Already?" He yawned again.

"Big doings." The Clerk ran his expert finger down the traffic-control sheet. "They're adjusting Sector T137 this morning. Starting at exactly nine o'clock." He glanced at his pocket watch. "Three hour alteration. Will finish by noon."

"T137? That's not far from here."

The Clerk's thin lips twisted with contempt. "Indeed. You're showing astonishing perspicacity, my black-haired friend. Maybe you can divine why I'm here."

"We overlap with T137."

"Exactly. Elements from this Sector are involved. We must make sure they're properly placed when the adjustment begins." The Clerk glanced toward the small green stucco house. "Your particular task concerns the man in there. He is employed by a business establishment lying within Sector T137. It's essential that he be there before nine o'clock."

The dog studied the house. The shades had been let up. The kitchen light was on. Beyond the lace curtains dim shapes could be seen, stirring around the table. A man and woman. They were drinking coffee.

"There they are," the dog murmured. "The man, you say? He's not going to be harmed, is he?"

"Of course not. But he must be at his office early. Usually he doesn't leave until after nine. Today he must leave at eight-thirty. He must be within Sector T137 before the process begins, or he won't be altered to coincide with the new adjustment."

The dog sighed. "That means I have to summon."

"Correct." The Clerk checked his instruction sheet. "You're to summon at precisely eight-fifteen. You've got that? Eight-fifteen. No later."

"What will an eight-fifteen summons bring?"

The Clerk flipped open his instruction book, examining the code columns. "It will bring A Friend with a Car. To drive him to work early." He closed the book and folded his arms, preparing to wait. "That way he'll get to his office almost an hour ahead of time. Which is vital."

"Vital," the dog murmured. He lay down, half inside his shed. His eyes closed. "Vital."

"Wake up! This must be done exactly on time. If you summon too soon or too late—"

The dog nodded sleepily. "I know. I'll do it right. I *always* do it right."

Ed Fletcher poured more cream in his coffee. He sighed, leaning back in his chair. Behind him the oven hissed softly, filling the kitchen with warm fumes. The yellow overhead light beamed down.

"Another roll?" Ruth asked.

"I'm full." Ed sipped his coffee. "You can have it."

"Have to go." Ruth got to her feet, unfastening her robe. "Time to go to work."

"Already?"

"Sure. You lucky bum! Wish I could sit around." Ruth moved toward the bathroom, running her fingers through her long black hair. "When you work for the Government you start early."

"But you get off early," Ed pointed out. He unfolded

the *Chronicle,* examining the sporting green. "Well, have a good time today. Don't type any wrong words, any double-entendres."

The bathroom door closed, as Ruth shed her robe and began dressing.

Ed yawned and glanced up at the clock over the sink. Plenty of time. Not even eight. He sipped more coffee and then rubbed his stubbled chin. He would have to shave. He shrugged lazily. Ten minutes, maybe.

Ruth came bustling out in her nylon slip, hurrying into the bedroom. "I'm late." She rushed rapidly around, getting into her blouse and skirt, her stockings, her little white shoes. Finally she bent over and kissed him. "Good-bye, honey. I'll do the shopping tonight."

"Good-bye." Ed lowered his newspaper and put his arm around his wife's trim waist, hugging her affectionately. "You smell nice. Don't flirt with the boss."

Ruth ran out the front door, clattering down the steps. He heard the click of her heels diminish down the sidewalk.

She was gone. The house was silent. He was alone.

Ed got to his feet, pushing his chair back. He wandered lazily into the bathroom and got his razor down. Eight-ten. He washed his face, rubbing it down with shaving cream, and began to shave. He shaved leisurely. He had plenty of time.

The Clerk bent over his round pocket watch, licking his lips nervously. Sweat stood out on his forehead. The second hand ticked on. Eight-fourteen. Almost time.

"Get ready!" the Clerk snapped. He tensed, his small body rigid. "Ten seconds to go!"

"Time!" the Clerk cried.

Nothing happened.

The Clerk turned, eyes wide with horror. From the little shed a thick black tail showed. The dog had gone back to sleep.

"TIME!" the Clerk shrieked. He kicked wildly at the furry rump. "In the name of God—"

The dog stirred. He thumped around hastily, backing out of the shed. "My goodness." Embarrassed, he made his way quickly to the fence. Standing up on his hind paws, he open his mouth wide. "Woof!" he summoned. He glanced apologetically at the Clerk. "I beg your pardon. I can't understand how—"

The Clerk gazed fixedly down at his watch. Cold terror knotted his stomach. The hands showed eight-sixteen. "You failed," he grated. "You failed! You miserable flea-bitten rag-bag of a wornout old mutt! You failed!"

The dog dropped and came anxiously back. "I failed, you say? You mean the summons time was—?"

"You summoned too late." The Clerk put his watch away slowly, a glazed expression on his face. "You summoned too late. We won't get A Friend with a Car. There's no telling what will come instead. I'm afraid to see what eight-sixteen brings."

"I hope he'll be in Sector T137 in time."

"He won't," the Clerk wailed. "He won't be there. We've made a mistake. We've made things go wrong!"

Ed was rinsing the shaving cream from his face when the muffled sound of the dog's bark echoed through the silent house.

"Damn," Ed muttered. "Wake up the whole block." He dried his face, listening. Was somebody coming?

A vibration. Then—

The doorbell rang.

Ed came out of the bathroom. Who could it be? Had Ruth forgotten something? He tossed on a white shirt and opened the front door.

A bright young man, face bland and eager, beamed happily at him. "Good morning, sir." He tipped his hat. "I'm sorry to bother you so early—"

"What do you want?"

"I'm from the Federal Life Insurance Company. I'm here to see you about—"

Ed pushed the door closed. "Don't want any. I'm in a rush. Have to get to work."

"Your wife said this was the only time I could catch you." The young man picked up his briefcase, easing the door open again. "She especially asked me to come this early. We don't usually begin our work at this time, but since she asked me, I made a special note about it."

"OK." Sighing wearily, Ed admitted the young man. "You can explain your policy while I get dressed."

The young man opened his briefcase on the couch, laying out heaps of pamphlets and illustrated folders. "I'd like to show you some of these figures, if I may. It's of great importance to you and your family to—"

Ed found himself sitting down, going over the pamphlets. He purchased a ten-thousand-dollar policy on his own life and then eased the young man out. He looked at the clock. Practically nine-thirty!

"Damn." He'd be late to work. He finished fastening his tie, grabbed his coat, turned off the oven and the lights, dumped the dishes in the sink, and ran out on the porch.

As he hurried toward the bus stop he was cursing inwardly. Life insurance salesmen. Why did the jerk have to come just as he was getting ready to leave?

Ed groaned. No telling what the consequences would be, getting to the office late. He wouldn't get there until almost ten. He set himself in anticipation. A sixth sense told him he was in for it. Something bad. It was the wrong day to be late.

If only the salesman hadn't come.

Ed hopped off the bus a block from his office. He began walking rapidly. The huge clock in front of Stein's Jewelry Store told him it was almost ten.

His heart sank. Old Douglas would give him hell for sure. He could see it now. Douglas puffing and blowing, red-faced, waving his thick finger at him; Miss Evans, smiling behind her typewriter; Jackie, the office boy, grinning and snickering; Earl Hendricks; Joe and Tom; Mary, dark-eyed, full bosom and long lashes. All of them, kidding him the whole rest of the day.

He came to the corner and stopped for the light. On the other side of the street rose the big white concrete building, the towering column of steel and cement, girders and glass windows—the office building. Ed flinched. Maybe he could say the elevator got stuck. Somewhere between the second and third floor.

The street light changed. Nobody else was crossing. Ed crossed alone. He hopped up on the curb on the far side—

And stopped, rigid.

The sun had winked off. One moment it was beaming

down. Then it was gone. Ed looked sharply up. Gray clouds swirled above him. Huge, formless clouds. Nothing more. An ominous, thick haze that made everything waver and dim. Uneasy chills plucked at him. *What was it?*

He advanced cautiously, feeling his way through the mist. Everything was silent. No sounds—not even the traffic sounds. Ed peered frantically around, trying to see through the rolling haze. No people. No cars. No sun. Nothing.

The office building loomed up ahead, ghostly. It was an indistinct gray. He put out his hand uncertainly—

A section of the building fell away. It rained down, a torrent of particles. Like sand. Ed gaped foolishly. A cascade of gray debris, spilling around his feet. And where he had touched the building, a jagged cavity yawned—an ugly pit marring the concrete.

Dazed, he made his way to the front steps. He mounted them. The steps gave way underfoot. His feet sank down. He was wading through shifting sand, weak, rotted stuff that broke under his weight.

He got into the lobby. The lobby was dim and obscure. The overhead lights flickered feebly in the gloom. An unearthly pall hung over everything.

He spied the cigar stand. The seller leaned silently, resting on the counter, toothpick between his teeth, his face vacant. *And gray*. He was gray all over.

"Hey," Ed croaked. "What's going on?"

The seller did not answer. Ed reached out toward him. His hand touched the seller's gray arm—and passed right through.

"Good God," Ed said.

The seller's arm came loose. It fell to the lobby floor, disintegrating into fragments. Bits of gray fiber. Like dust. Ed's senses reeled.

"Help!" he shouted, finding his voice.

No answer. He peered around. A few shapes stood here and there: a man reading a newspaper, two women waiting at the elevator.

Ed made his way over to the man. He reached out and touched him.

The man slowly collapsed. He settled into a heap, a loose pile of gray ash. Dust. Particles. The two women dissolved when he touched them. Silently. They made no sound as they broke apart.

Ed found the stairs. He grabbed hold of the bannister and climbed. The stairs collapsed under him. He hurried faster. Behind him lay a broken path—his footprints clearly visible in the concrete. Clouds of ash blew around him as he reached the second floor.

He gazed down the silent corridor. He saw more clouds of ash. He heard no sound. There was just darkness—rolling darkness.

He climbed unsteadily to the third floor. Once, his shoe broke completely through the stair. For a sickening second he hung, poised over a yawning hole that looked down into a bottomless nothing.

Then he climbed on, and emerged in front of his own office: DOUGLAS AND BLAKE, REAL ESTATE.

The hall was dim, gloomy with clouds of ash. The overhead lights flickered fitfully. He reached for the door handle. The handle came off in his hand. He dropped it and dug his fingernails into the door. The plate glass crashed past him, breaking into bits. He tore the door open and stepped over it, into the office.

Miss Evans sat at her typewriter, fingers resting quietly on the keys. She did not move. She was gray, her hair, her skin, her clothing. She was without color. Ed touched her. His fingers went through her shoulder, into dry flakiness.

He drew back, sickened. Miss Evans did not stir.

He moved on. He pushed against a desk. The desk collapsed into rotting dust. Earl Hendricks stood by the water cooler, a cup in his hand. He was a gray statue, unmoving. Nothing stirred. No sound. No life. The whole office was gray dust—without life or motion.

Ed found himself out in the corridor again. He shook his head, dazed. What did it mean? Was he going out of his mind? Was he—?

A sound.

Ed turned, peering into the gray mist. A creature was coming, hurrying rapidly. A man—a man in a white robe. Behind him others came. Men in white, with equipment. They were lugging complex machinery.

"Hey—" Ed gasped weakly.

The men stopped. Their mouths opened. Their eyes popped.

"Look!"

"Something's gone wrong!"

"One still charged."

"Get the de-energizer."

"We can't proceed until—"

The men came toward Ed, moving around him. One lugged a long hose with some sort of nozzle. A portable cart came wheeling up. Instructions were rapidly shouted.

Ed broke out of his paralysis. Fear swept over him. Panic. Something hideous was happening. He had to get out. Warn people. Get away.

He turned and ran, back down the stairs. The stairs collapsed under him. He fell half a flight, rolling in heaps of dry ash. He got to his feet and hurried on, down to the ground floor.

The lobby was lost in the clouds of gray ash. He pushed blindly through, toward the door. Behind him, the white-clad men were coming, dragging their equipment and shouting to each other, hurrying quickly after him.

He reached the sidewalk. Behind him the office building wavered and sagged, sinking to one side, torrents of ash raining down in heaps. He raced toward the corner, the men just behind him. Gray clouds swirled around him. He groped his way across the street, hands outstretched. He gained the opposite curb—

The sun winked on. Warm yellow sunlight streamed down on him. Cars honked. Traffic lights changed. On all sides men and women in bright spring clothes hurried and pushed: shoppers, a blue-clad cop, salesmen with briefcases. Stores, windows, signs . . . noisy cars moving up and down the street. . . .

And overhead was the bright sun and familiar blue sky.

Ed halted, gasping for breath. He turned and looked back the way he had come. Across the street was the office building—as it had always been. Firm and distinct. Concrete and glass and steel.

He stepped back a pace and collided with a hurrying citizen. "Hey," the man grunted. "Watch it."

"Sorry." Ed shook his head, trying to clear it. From where he stood, the office building looked like always, big and solemn and substantial, rising up imposingly on the other side of the street.

But a minute ago—

Maybe he was out of his mind. He had seen the building crumbling into dust. Building—and people. They had fallen into gray clouds of dust. And the men in white—they had chased him. Men in white robes, shouting orders, wheeling complex equipment.

He was out of his mind. There was no other explanation. Weakly, Ed turned and stumbled along the sidewalk, his mind reeling. He moved blindly, without purpose, lost in a haze of confusion and terror.

The Clerk was brought into the top-level Administrative chambers and told to wait.

He paced back and forth nervously, clasping and wringing his hands in an agony of apprehension. He took off his glasses and wiped them shakily.

Lord. All the trouble and grief. And it wasn't his fault. But he would have to take the rap. It was his responsibility to get the Summoners routed out and their instructions followed. The miserable flea-infested Summoner had gone back to sleep—and *he* would have to answer for it.

The doors opened. "All right," a voice murmured, preoccupied. It was a tired, care-worn voice. The Clerk trembled and entered slowly, sweat dripping down his neck into his celluloid collar.

The Old Man glanced up, laying aside his book. He studied the Clerk calmly, his faded blue eyes mild—a deep, ancient mildness that made the Clerk tremble even more. He took out his handkerchief and mopped his brow.

"I understand there was a mistake," the Old Man murmured. "In connection with Sector T137. Something to do with an element from an adjoining area."

"That's right." The Clerk's voice was faint and husky. "Very unfortunate."

"What exactly occurred?"

"I started out this morning with my instruction sheets. The material relating to T137 had top priority, of course. I served notice on the Summoner in my area that an eight-fifteen summons was required."

"Did the Summoner understand the urgency?"

"Yes, sir." The Clerk hesitated. "But—"

"But what?"

The Clerk twisted miserably. "While my back was turned the Summoner crawled back in his shed and went to sleep. I was occupied, checking the exact time with my watch. I called the moment—but there was no response."

"You called at eight-fifteen exactly?"

"Yes, sir! Exactly eight-fifteen. But the Summoner was asleep. By the time I managed to arouse him it was eight-*sixteen*. He summoned, but instead of A Friend with a Car we got a—A Life Insurance Salesman." The Clerk's face screwed up with disgust. "The Salesman kept the element there until almost nine-thirty. Therefore he was late to work instead of early."

For a moment the Old Man was silent. "Then the element was not within T137 when the adjustment began."

"No. He arrived about ten o'clock."

"During the middle of the adjustment." The Old Man got to his feet and paced slowly back and forth, face grim, hands behind his back. His long robe flowed out behind him. "A serious matter. During a Sector Adjustment all related elements from other Sectors must be included. Otherwise, their orientations remain out of phase. When this element entered T137 the adjustment had been in progress fifty minutes. The element encountered the Sector at its most de-energized stage. He wandered about until one of the adjustment teams met him."

"Did they catch him?"

"Unfortunately no. He fled, out of the Sector. Into a nearby fully energized area."

"What—what then?"

The Old Man stopped pacing, his lined face grim. He ran a heavy hand through his long white hair. "We do not know. We lost contact with him. We will reestablish contact soon, of course. But for the moment he is out of control."

"What are you going to do?"

"He must be contacted and contained. He must be brought up here. There's no other solution."

"Up *here!*"

"It is too late to de-energize him. By the time he is regained he will have told others. To wipe his mind clean would only complicate matters. Usual methods will not suffice. I must deal with this problem myself."

"I hope he's located quickly," the Clerk said.

"He will be. Every Watcher is alerted. Every Watcher and every Summoner." The Old Man's eyes twinkled. "Even the Clerks, although we hesitate to count on them."

The Clerk flushed. "I'll be glad when this thing is over," he muttered.

Ruth came tripping down the stairs and out of the building, into the hot noonday sun. She lit a cigarette and hurried along the walk, her small bosom rising and falling as she breathed in the spring air.

"Ruth." Ed stepped up behind her.

"Ed!" She spun, gasping in astonishment. "What are you doing away from—?"

"Come on." Ed grabbed her arm, pulling her along. "Let's keep moving."

"But what—?"

"I'll tell you later." Ed's face was pale and grim. "Let's go where we can talk. In private."

"I was going down to have lunch at Louie's. We can talk there." Ruth hurried along breathlessly. "What is it? What's happened? You look so strange. And why aren't you at work? Did you—did you get fired?"

They crossed the street and entered a small restaurant. Men and women milled around, getting their lunch. Ed found a table in the back, secluded in a corner. "Here." He sat down abruptly. "This will do." She slid into the other chair.

Ed ordered a cup of coffee. Ruth had salad and creamed tuna on toast, coffee and peach pie. Silently, Ed watched her as she ate, his face dark and moody.

"Please tell me," Ruth begged.

"You really want to know?"

"Of course I want to know!" Ruth put her small hand anxiously on his. "I'm your wife."

"Something happened today. This morning. I was late to work. A damn insurance man came by and held me up. I was half an hour late."

Ruth caught her breath. "Douglas fired you."

"No." Ed ripped a paper napkin slowly into bits. He

stuffed the bits in the half-empty water glass. "I was worried as hell. I got off the bus and hurried down the street. I noticed it when I stepped up on the curb in front of the office."

"Noticed what?"

Ed told her. The whole works. Everything.

When he had finished, Ruth sat back, her face white, hands trembling. "I see," she murmured. "No wonder you're upset." She drank a little cold coffee, the cup rattling against the saucer. "What a terrible thing."

Ed leaned intently toward his wife. "Ruth. Do you think I'm going crazy?"

Ruth's red lips twisted. "I don't know what to say. It's so strange. . . ."

"Yeah. Strange is hardly the word for it. I poked my hands right through them. Like they were clay. Old dry clay. Dust. Dust figures." Ed lit a cigarette from Ruth's pack. "When I got out I looked back and there it was. The office building. Like always."

"You were afraid Mr. Douglas would bawl you out, weren't you?"

"Sure. I was afraid—and guilty." Ed's eyes flickered. "I know what you're thinking. I was late and I couldn't face him. So I had some sort of protective psychotic fit. Retreat from reality." He stubbed the cigarette out savagely. "Ruth, I've been wandering around town since. Two and a half hours. Sure, I'm afraid. I'm afraid like hell to go back."

"Of Douglas?"

"No! The men in white." Ed shuddered. "God. Chasing me. With their damn hoses and—and equipment."

Ruth was silent. Finally she looked up at her husband, her dark eyes bright. "You have to go back, Ed."

"Back? Why?"

"To prove something."

"Prove what?"

"Prove it's all right." Ruth's hand pressed against his. "You have to, Ed. You have to go back and face it. To show yourself there's nothing to be afraid of."

"The hell with it! After what I saw? Listen, Ruth. I saw the fabric of reality split open. I saw—*behind*. Underneath. I saw what was really there. And I don't want to go back. I don't want to see dust people again. Ever."

Ruth's eyes were fixed intently on him. "I'll go back with you," she said.

"For God's sake."

"For *your* sake. For your sanity. So you'll know." Ruth got abruptly to her feet, pulling her coat around her. "Come on, Ed. I'll go with you. We'll go up there together. To the office of Douglas and Blake, Real Estate. I'll even go in with you to see Mr. Douglas."

Ed got up slowly, staring hard at his wife. "You think I blacked out. Cold feet. Couldn't face the boss." His voice was low and strained. "Don't you?"

Ruth was already threading her way toward the cashier. "Come on. You'll see. It'll all be there. Just like it always was."

"OK," Ed said. He followed her slowly. "We'll go back there—and see which of us is right."

They crossed the street together, Ruth holding on tight to Ed's arm. Ahead of them was the building, the towering structure of concrete and metal and glass.

"There it is," Ruth said. "See?"

There it was, all right. The big building rose up, firm and solid, glittering in the early afternoon sun, its windows sparkling brightly.

Ed and Ruth stepped up onto the curb. Ed tensed himself, his body rigid. He winced as his foot touched the pavement—

But nothing happened: the street noises continued; cars, people hurrying past; a kid selling papers. There were sounds, smells, the noises of the city in the middle of the day. And overhead was the sun and the bright blue sky.

"See?" Ruth said. "I was right."

They walked up the front steps, into the lobby. Behind the cigar stand the seller stood, arms folded, listening to the ball game. "Hi, Mr. Fletcher," he called to Ed. His face lit up good-naturedly. "Who's the dame? Your wife know about this?"

Ed laughed unsteadily. They passed on toward the elevator. Four or five businessmen stood waiting. They were middle-aged men, well dressed, waiting impatiently in a bunch. "Hey, Fletcher," one said. "Where you been all day? Douglas is yelling his head off."

"Hello, Earl," Ed muttered. He gripped Ruth's arm. "Been a little sick."

The elevator came. They got in. The elevator rose. "Hi, Ed," the elevator operator said. "Who's the good-looking gal? Why don't you introduce her around?"

Ed grinned mechanically. "My wife."

The elevator let them off at the third floor. Ed and Ruth got out, heading toward the glass door of Douglas and Blake, Real Estate.

Ed halted, breathing shallowly. "Wait." He licked his lips. "I—"

Ruth waited calmly as Ed wiped his forehead and neck with his handkerchief. "All right now?"

"Yeah." Ed moved forward. He pulled open the glass door.

Miss Evans glanced up, ceasing her typing. "Ed Fletcher! Where on earth have you been?"

"I've been sick. Hello, Tom."

Tom glanced up from his work. "Hi, Ed. Say, Douglas is yelling for your scalp. Where have you been?"

"I know." Ed turned wearily to Ruth. "I guess I better go in and face the music."

Ruth squeezed his arm. "You'll be all right. I know." She smiled, a relieved flash of white teeth and red lips. "OK? Call me if you need me."

"Sure." Ed kissed her briefly on the mouth. "Thanks, honey. Thanks a lot. I don't know what the hell went wrong with me. I guess it's over."

"Forget it. So long." Ruth skipped back out of the office, the door closing after her. Ed listened to her race down the hall to the elevator.

"Nice little gal," Jackie said appreciatively.

"Yeah." Ed nodded, straightening his necktie. He moved unhappily toward the inner office, steeling himself. Well, he had to face it. Ruth was right. But he was going to have a hell of a time explaining it to the boss. He could see Douglas now, thick red wattles, big bull roar, face distorted with rage—

Ed stopped abruptly at the entrance to the inner office. He froze rigid. The inner office—it was *changed.*

The hackles of his neck rose. Cold fear gripped him, clutching at his windpipe. The inner office was different. He turned his head slowly, taking in the sight: the desks, chairs, fixtures, file cabinets, pictures.

Changes. Little changes. Subtle. Ed closed his eyes and opened them slowly. He was alert, breathing rapidly, his pulse racing. It was changed, all right. No doubt about it.

"What's the matter, Ed?" Tom asked. The staff watched him curiously, pausing in their work.

Ed said nothing. He advanced slowly into the inner office. The office had been *gone over.* He could tell. Things had been altered. Rearranged. Nothing obvious—nothing he could put his finger on. But he could tell.

Joe Kent greeted him uneasily. "What's the matter, Ed? You look like a wild dog. Is something—?"

Ed studied Joe. He was different. Not the same. What was it?

Joe's face. It was a little fuller. His shirt was blue-striped. Joe never wore blue stripes. Ed examined Joe's desk. He saw papers and accounts. The desk—it was too far to the right. And it was bigger. It wasn't the same desk.

The picture on the wall. It wasn't the same. It was a different picture entirely. And the things on top of the file cabinet—some were new, others were gone.

He looked back through the door. Now that he thought about it, Miss Evans' hair was different, done a different way. And it was lighter.

In here, Mary, filing her nails, over by the window—she was taller, fuller. Her purse, lying on the desk in front of her—a red purse, red knit.

"You always . . . have that purse?" Ed demanded.

Mary glanced up. "What?"

"That purse. You always have that?"

Mary laughed. She smoothed her skirt coyly around her shapely thighs, her long lashes blinking modestly. "Why, Mr. Fletcher. What do you mean?"

Ed turned away. *He knew.* Even if she didn't. She had been redone—changed: her purse, her clothes, her figure, everything about her. None of them knew—but him. His mind spun dizzily. They were all changed. All of them were different. They had all been remolded, recast. Subtly—but it was there.

The wastebasket. It was smaller, not the same. The window shades—white, not ivory. The wall paper was not the same pattern. The lighting fixtures. . . .

Endless, subtle changes.

Ed made his way back to the inner office. He lifted his hand and knocked on Douglas' door.

"Come in."

Ed pushed the door open. Nathan Douglas looked up impatiently. "Mr. Douglas—" Ed began. He came into the room unsteadily—and stopped.

Douglas was not the same. Not at all. His whole office was changed: the rugs, the drapes. The desk was oak, not mahogany. And Douglas himself. . . .

Douglas was younger, thinner. His hair, brown. His skin not so red. His face smoother. No wrinkles. Chin reshaped. Eyes green, not black. He was a different man. But still Douglas—a different Douglas. A different version!

"What is it?" Douglas demanded impatiently. "Oh, it's you, Fletcher. Where were you this morning?"

Ed backed out. Fast.

He slammed the door and hurried back through the inner office. Tom and Miss Evans glanced up, startled. Ed passed by them, grabbing the hall door open.

"Hey!" Tom called. "What—?"

Ed hurried down the hall. Terror leaped through him. He had to hurry. He had *seen*. There wasn't much time. He came to the elevator and stabbed the button.

No time.

He ran to the stairs and started down. He reached the second floor. His terror grew. It was a matter of seconds.

Seconds!

The public phone. Ed ran into the phone booth. He dragged the door shut after him. Wildly, he dropped a dime in the slot and dialed. He had to call the police. He held the receiver to his ear, his heart pounding.

Warn them. Changes. Somebody tampering with reality. Altering it. He had been right. The white-clad men . . . their equipment . . . going through the building.

"Hello!" Ed shouted hoarsely. There was no answer. No hum. Nothing.

Ed peered frantically out the door.

And he sagged, defeated. Slowly he hung up the telephone receiver.

He was no longer on the second floor. The phone booth was rising, leaving the second floor behind, carrying him up, faster and faster. It rose floor by floor, moving silently, swiftly.

The phone booth passed through the ceiling of the building and out into the bright sunlight. It gained speed. The ground fell away below. Buildings and streets were getting smaller each moment. Tiny specks hurried along, far below, cars and people, dwindling rapidly.

Clouds drifted between him and the earth. Ed shut his eyes, dizzy with fright. He held on desperately to the door handles of the phone booth.

Faster and faster the phone booth climbed. The earth was rapidly being left behind, far below.

Ed peered up wildly. *Where?* Where was he going? Where was it taking him?

He stood gripping the door handles, waiting.

The Clerk nodded curtly. "That's him, all right. The element in question."

Ed Fletcher looked around him. He was in a huge chamber. The edges fell away into indistinct shadows. In front of him stood a man with notes and ledgers under his arm, peering at him through steel-rimmed glasses. He was a nervous little man, sharp-eyed, with celluloid collar, blue serge suit, vest, watch chain. He wore black shiny shoes.

And beyond him—

An old man sat quietly, in an immense modern chair. He watched Fletcher calmly, his blue eyes mild and tired. A strange thrill shot through Fletcher. It was not fear. Rather it was a vibration, rattling his bones—a deep sense of awe, tinged with fascination.

"Where—what is this place?" he asked faintly. He was still dazed from his quick ascent.

"Don't ask questions!" the nervous little man snapped angrily, tapping his pencil against his ledgers. "You're here to answer, not ask."

The Old Man moved a little. He raised his hand. "I will speak to the element alone," he murmured. His voice was low. It vibrated and rumbled through the chamber. Again the wave of fascinated awe swept Ed.

"Alone?" The little fellow backed away, gathering his books and papers in his arms. "Of course." He glanced hostilely at Ed Fletcher. "I'm glad he's finally in custody. All the work and trouble just for—"

He disappeared through a door. The door closed softly behind him. Ed and the Old Man were alone.

"Please sit down," the Old Man said.

Ed found a seat. He sat down awkwardly, nervously. He got out his cigarettes and then put them away again.

"What's wrong?" the Old Man asked.

"I'm just beginning to understand."

"Understand what?"

"That I'm dead."

The Old Man smiled briefly. "Dead? No, you're not dead. You're . . . visiting. An unusual event, but necessitated by circumstances." He leaned toward Ed. "Mr. Fletcher, you have got yourself involved in something."

"Yeah," Ed agreed. "I wish I knew what it was. Or how it happened."

"It was not your fault. You're the victim of a clerical error. A mistake was made—not by you. But involving you."

"What mistake?" Ed rubbed his forehead wearily. "I—I got in on something. I saw *through*. I saw something I wasn't supposed to see."

The Old Man nodded. "That's right. You saw something you were not supposed to see—something few elements have been aware of, let alone witnessed."

"Elements?"

"An official term. Let it pass. A mistake was made, but we hope to rectify it. It is my hope that—"

"Those people," Ed interrupted. "Heaps of dry ash. And gray. Like they were dead. Only it was everything: the stairs and walls and floor. No color or life."

"That Sector had been temporarily de-energized. So the adjustment team could enter and effect changes."

"Changes." Ed nodded. "That's right. When I went back later, everything was alive again. But not the same. It was all different."

"The adjustment was complete by noon. The team finished its work and re-energized the Sector."

"I see," Ed muttered.

"You were supposed to have been in the Sector when the adjustment began. Because of an error you were not. You came into the Sector late—during the adjustment itself. You fled, and when you returned it was over. You saw, and you should not have seen. Instead of a witness you should have been part of the adjustment. Like the others, you should have undergone changes."

Sweat came out on Ed Fletcher's head. He wiped it away. His stomach turned over. Weakly, he cleared his throat. "I get the picture." His voice was almost inaudible. A chilling premonition moved through him. "I was supposed to be changed like the others. But I guess something went wrong."

"Something went wrong. An error occurred. And now a serious problem exists. You have seen these things. You know a great deal. And you are not coordinated with the new configuration."

"Gosh," Ed muttered. "Well, I won't tell anybody." Cold sweat poured off him. "You can count on that. I'm as good as changed."

"You have already told someone," the Old Man said coldly.

"Me?" Ed blinked. "Who?"

"Your wife."

Ed trembled. The color drained from his face, leaving it sickly white. "That's right. I did."

"Your wife knows." The Old Man's face twisted angrily. "A woman. Of all the things to tell—"

"I didn't know." Ed retreated, panic leaping through him. "But I know *now*. You can count on me. Consider me changed."

The ancient blue eyes bored keenly into him, peering far into his depths. "And you were going to call the police. You wanted to inform the authorities."

"But I didn't know *who* was doing the changing."

"Now you know. The natural process must be supplemented—adjusted here and there. Corrections must be made. We are fully licensed to make such corrections. Our adjustment teams perform vital work."

Ed plucked up a measure of courage. "This particular adjustment. Douglas. The office. What was it for? I'm sure it was some worthwhile purpose."

The Old Man waved his hand. Behind him in the shadows an immense map glowed into existence. Ed caught his breath. The edges of the map faded off in obscurity. He saw an infinite web of detailed sections, a network of squares and ruled lines. Each square was marked. Some glowed with a blue light. The lights altered constantly.

"The Sector Board," the Old Man said. He sighed wearily. "A staggering job. Sometimes we wonder how we can go on another period. But it must be done. For the good of all. For *your* good."

"The change. In our—our Sector."

"Your office deals in real estate. The old Douglas was a shrewd man, but rapidly becoming infirm. His physical health was waning. In a few days Douglas will be offered a chance to purchase a large unimproved forest area in western Canada. It will require most of his assets. The older, less virile Douglas would have hesitated. It is imperative he not hesitate. He must purchase the area and clear the land at once. Only a younger man—a younger Douglas—would undertake this.

"When the land is cleared, certain anthropological remains will be discovered. They have already been placed there. Douglas will lease his land to the Canadian Government for scientific study. The remains found there will cause international excitement in learned circles.

"A chain of events will be set in motion. Men from numerous countries will come to Canada to examine the remains. Soviet, Polish, and Czech scientists will make the journey.

"The chain of events will draw these scientists together for the first time in years. National research will be temporarily forgotten in the excitement of these nonnational discoveries. One of the leading Soviet scientists will make friends with a Belgian scientist. Before they depart they will agree to correspond—without the knowledge of their governments, of course.

"The circle will widen. Other scientists on both sides will be drawn in. A society will be founded. More and more educated men will transfer an increasing amount of time to this international society. Purely national research will suffer a slight but extremely critical eclipse. The war tension will somewhat wane.

"This alteration is vital. And it is dependent on the purchase and clearing of the section of wilderness in Canada. The old Douglas would not have dared take the risk. But the altered Douglas, and his altered, more youthful staff, will pursue this work with wholehearted enthusiasm. And from this, the vital chain of widening events will come about. The beneficiaries will be *you*. Our methods may seem strange and indirect. Even incomprehensible. But I assure you we know what we're doing."

"I know that now," Ed said.

"So you do. You know a great deal. Much too much. No element should posssess such knowledge. I should perhaps call an adjustment team in here. . . ."

A picture formed in Ed's mind: swirling gray clouds, gray men and women. He shuddered. "Look," he croaked. "I'll do anything. Anything at all. Only don't de-energize me." Sweat ran down his face. "OK?"

The Old Man pondered. "Perhaps some alternative could be found. There is another possibility. . . ."

"What?" Ed asked eagerly. "What is it?"

The Old Man spoke slowly, thoughtfully. "If I allow you to return, you will swear never to speak of the matter? Will you swear not to reveal to anyone the things you saw? The things you know?"

"Sure!" Ed gasped eagerly, blinding relief flooding over him. "I swear!"

"Your wife. She must know nothing more. She must think it was only a passing psychological fit—retreat from reality."

"She thinks that already."

"She must continue to."

Ed set his jaw firmly. "I'll see that she continues to think it was a mental aberration. She'll never know what really happened."

"You are certain you can keep the truth from her?"

"Sure," Ed said confidently. "I know I can."

"All right." The Old Man nodded slowly. "I will send you back. But you must tell no one." He swelled visibly.

"Remember: you will eventually come back to me—everyone does, in the end—and your fate will not be enviable."

"I won't tell her," Ed said, sweating. "I promise. You have my word on that. I can handle Ruth. Don't give it a second thought."

Ed arrived home at sunset.

He blinked, dazed from the rapid descent. For a moment he stood on the pavement, regaining his balance and catching his breath. Then he walked quickly up the path.

He pushed the door open and entered the little green stucco house.

"Ed!" Ruth came flying, face distorted with tears. She threw her arms around him, hugging him tight. "Where the hell have you been?"

"Been?" Ed murmured. "At the office, of course."

Ruth pulled back abruptly. "No, you haven't."

Vague tendrils of alarm plucked at Ed. "Of course I have. Where else—?"

"I called Douglas about three. He said you left. You walked out, practically as soon as I turned my back. Eddie—"

Ed patted her nervously. "Take it easy, honey." He began unbuttoning his coat. "Everything's OK. Understand? Things are perfectly all right."

Ruth sat down on the arm of the couch. She blew her nose, dabbing at her eyes. "If you knew how much I've worried." She put her handkerchief away and folded her arms. "I want to know where you were."

Uneasily, Ed hung his coat in the closet. He came over and kissed her. Her lips were ice cold. "I'll tell you all about it. But what do you say we have something to eat? I'm starved."

Ruth studied him intently. She got down from the arm of the couch. "I'll change and fix dinner."

She hurried into the bedroom and slipped off her shoes and nylons. Ed followed her. "I didn't mean to worry you," he said carefully. "After you left me today I realized you were right."

"Oh?" Ruth unfastened her blouse and skirt, arranging them over a hanger. "Right about what?"

"About me." He manufactured a grin and made it glow across his face. "About . . . what happened."

Ruth hung her slip over the hanger. She studied her husband intently as she struggled into her tight-fitting jeans. "Go on."

The moment had come. It was now or never. Ed Fletcher braced himself and chose his words carefully. "I realized," he stated, "that the whole darn thing was in my mind. You were right, Ruth. Completely right. And I even realize what caused it."

Ruth rolled her cotton T-shirt down and tucked it in her jeans. "What was the cause?"

"Overwork."

"Overwork?"

"I need a vacation. I haven't had a vacation in years. My mind isn't on my job. I've been daydreaming." He said it firmly, but his heart was in his mouth. "I need to get away. To the mountains. Bass fishing. Or—" He searched his mind frantically. "Or—"

Ruth came toward him ominously. "Ed!" she said sharply. "Look at me!"

"What's the matter?" Panic shot through him. "Why are you looking at me like that?"

"Where were you this afternoon?"

Ed's grin faded. "I told you. I went for a walk. Didn't I tell you? A walk. To think things over."

"Don't lie to me, Eddie Fletcher! I can tell when you're lying!" Fresh tears welled up in Ruth's eyes. Her breasts rose and fell excitedly under her cotton shirt. "Admit it! You didn't go for a walk!"

Ed stammered weakly. Sweat poured off him. He sagged helplessly against the door. "What do you mean?"

Ruth's black eyes flashed with anger. "Come on! I want to know where you were! Tell me! I have a right to know. What really happened?"

Ed retreated in terror, his resolve melting like wax. It was going all wrong. "Honest. I went out for a—"

"Tell me!" Ruth's sharp fingernails dug into his arm. "I want to know where you were—and who you were with!"

Ed opened his mouth. He tried to grin, but his face failed to respond. "I don't know what you mean."

"You know what I mean. Who were you with? Where did you go? Tell me! I'll find out, sooner or later."

There was no way out. He was licked—and he knew it. He couldn't keep it from her. Desperately he stalled, praying for time. If he could only distract her, get her mind on something else. If she would only let up, even for a second. He could invent something—a better story. Time—he needed more time. "Ruth, you've got to—"

Suddenly there was a sound: the bark of a dog, echoing through the dark house.

Ruth let go, cocking her head alertly. "That was Dobbie. I think somebody's coming."

The doorbell rang.

"You stay here. I'll be right back." Ruth ran out of the room, to the front door. "Darn it." She pulled the front door open.

"Good evening!" The young man stepped quickly inside, loaded down with objects, grinning broadly at Ruth. "I'm from the Sweep-Rite Vacuum Cleaner Company."

Ruth scowled impatiently. "Really, we're about to sit down at the table."

"Oh, this will only take a moment." The young man set down the vacuum cleaner and its attachments with a metallic crash. Rapidly, he unrolled a long illustrated banner, showing the vacuum cleaner in action. "Now, if you'll just hold this while I plug in the cleaner—"

He bustled happily about, unplugging the TV set, plugging in the cleaner, pushing the chairs out of his way.

"I'll show you the drape scraper first." He attached a hose and nozzle to the big gleaming tank. "Now, if you'll just sit down I'll demonstrate each of these easy-to-use attachments." His happy voice rose over the roar of the cleaner. "You'll notice—"

Ed Fletcher sat down on the bed. He groped in his pocket until he found his cigarettes. Shakily he lit one and leaned back against the wall, weak with relief.

He gazed up, a look of gratitude on his face. "Thanks," he said softly. "I think we'll make it—after all. Thanks a lot."

PSI-MAN

HE was a lean man, middle-aged, with grease-stained hair and skin, a crumpled cigarette between his teeth, his left hand clamped around the wheel of his car. The car, an ex-commercial surface truck, rumbled noisily but smoothly as it ascended the outgoing ramp and approached the check-gate that terminated the commune area.

"Slow down," his wife said. "There's the guard sitting on that pile of crates."

Ed Garby rode the brake; the car settled grimly into a long glide that ended directly in front of the guard. In the back seat of the car the twins fretted restlessly, already bothered by the gummy heat oozing through the top and windows of the car. Down his wife's smooth neck great drops of perspiration slid. In her arms the baby twisted and struggled feebly.

"How's she?" Ed muttered to his wife, indicating the wad of gray, sickly flesh that poked from the soiled blanket. "Hot—like me."

The guard came strolling over indifferently, sleeves rolled up, rifle slung over his shoulder. "What say, mac?" Resting his big hands in the open window, he gazed dully into the interior of the car, observing the man and wife, the children, the dilapidated upholstery. "Going outside awhile? Let's see your pass."

Ed got out the crumpled pass and handed it over. "I got a sick child."

The guard examined the pass and returned it. "Better take her down to sixth level. You got a right to use the infirmary; you live in this dump like the rest of us."

"No," Ed said. "I'm taking no child of mine down to that butchery."

The guard shook his head in disagreement. "They got good equipment, mac. High-powered stuff left over from the war. Take her down there and they'll fix her up." He waved toward the desolate expanse of dry trees and hills that lay beyond the check-gate. "What do you think you'll find out there? You going to dump her somewhere? Toss her in a creek? Down a well? It's none of my business, but I wouldn't take a dog out there, let alone a sick child."

Ed started up the motor. "I'm getting help out there. Take a child down to sixth and they make her a laboratory animal. They experiment, cut her up, throw her away and say they couldn't save her. They got used to doing that in the war; they never stopped."

"Suit yourself," the guard said, moving away from the car. "Myself, I'd sooner trust military doctors with equipment than some crazy old quack living out in the ruins. Some savage heathen tie a bag of stinking dung around her neck, mumble nonsense and wave and dance around." He shouted furiously after the car: "Damn fools—going back to barbarism, when you got doctors and X-rays and serums down on sixth! Why the hell do you want to go out in the ruins when you've got a civilization here?"

He wandered glumly back to his crates. And added, "What there is left of it."

Arid land, as dry and parched as dead skin, lay on both sides of the rutted tracks that made up the road. A harsh rattle of noonday wind shook the gaunt trees jutting here and there from the cracked, baking soil. An occasional drab bird fluttered in the thick underbrush, heavy-set gray shapes that scratched peevishly in search of grubs.

Behind the car the white concrete walls of the commune faded and were lost in the distance. Ed Garby watched them go apprehensively; his hands convulsively jerked as a twist in the road cut off the radar towers posted on the hills overlooking the commune.

"Damn it," he muttered thickly, "maybe he was right; maybe we're making a mistake." Doubts shivered through his mind. The trip was dangerous; even heavily-armed scavenger parties were attacked by predatory animals and by the wild bands of quasi-humans living in the abandoned ruins littered across the planet. All he had to protect himself and his family was his hand-operated cutting tool. He knew how to use it, of course; didn't he grind it into a moving belt of reclaimed wreckage ten hours a day every day of the week? But if the motor of the car failed . . .

"Stop worrying," Barbara said quietly. "I've been along here before, and there's nothing ever gone wrong."

He felt shame and guilt: his wife had crept outside the commune many times, along with other women and wives; and with some of the men, too. A good part of the proletariat left the commune, with and without passes . . . anything to break the monotony of work and educational lectures. But his fear returned. It wasn't the physical menace that bothered him, or even unfamiliar separation from the vast submerged tank of steel and concrete in which he had been born and in which he had grown up, spent his life, worked and married. It was the realization that the guard had been right, that he was sinking into ignorance and superstition, that made his skin turn cold and clammy, in spite of the baking midsummer heat.

"Women always lead it," he said aloud. "Men built machines, organized science, cities. Women have their potions and brews. I guess we're seeing the end of reason. We're seeing the last remnants of rational society."

"What's a city?" one of the twins asked.

"You're seeing one now," Ed answered. He pointed beyond the road. "Take a good look."

The trees had ended. The baked surface of brown earth had faded to a dull metallic glint. An uneven plain stretched out, bleak and dismal, a pocked surface of jagged heaps and pits. Dark weeds grew here and there. An occasional wall remained standing; at one point a bathtub lay on its side like a dead, toothless mouth, deprived of face and head.

The region had been picked over countless times. Everything of value had been loaded up and trucked to the various communes in the area. Along the road were neat heaps of bones, collected but never utilized. Use had been found for cement rubble, iron scrap, wiring, plastic tubing, paper and cloth—but not for bones.

"You mean people lived *there?*" the twins protested simultaneously. Disbelief and horror showed on their faces. "It's—awful."

The road divided. Ed slowed the car down and waited for his wife to direct him. "Is it far?" he demanded hoarsely. "This place gives me the creeps. You can't tell what's hanging around in those cellars. We gassed them back in '09, but it's probably worn off by now."

"To the right," Barbara said. "Beyond that hill, there."

Ed shifted into low-low and edged the car past a ditch, onto a side road. "You really think this old woman has the power?" he asked helplessly. "I hear so damn much stuff—I never know what's true and what's hogwash. There's always supposed to be some old hag that can raise the dead and read the future and cure the sick. People've been reporting that stuff for five thousand years."

"And for five thousand years such things have been happening." His wife's voice was placid, confident. "They're always there to help us. All we have to do is go to them. I saw her heal Mary Fulsome's son; remember, he had that withered leg and couldn't walk. The medics wanted to destroy him."

"According to Mary Fulsome," Ed muttered harshly.

The car nosed its way between dead branches of ancient trees. The ruins fell behind; abruptly the road plunged into a gloomy thicket of vines and shrubs that shut out the sunlight. Ed blinked, then snapped on the dim headlights. They flickered on as the car ground its way up a rutted hill, around a narrow curve . . . and then the road ceased.

They had reached their destination. Four rusty cars blocked the road; others were parked on the shoulders and among the twisted trees. Beyond the cars stood a group of silent people, men and their families, in the drab uniforms of commune workers. Ed pulled on the brake and fumbled for the ignition key; he was astounded at the variety of communes represented. All the nearby communes, and distant ones he had never encountered. Some of the waiting people had come hundreds of miles.

"There's always people waiting," Barbara said. She kicked open the bent door and carefully slid out, the baby in her arms. "People come here for all kinds of help, whenever they're in need."

Beyond the crowd was a crude wooden building, shabby and dilapidated, a patched-together shelter of the war years. A gradual line of waiting persons was being conducted up the rickety steps and into the buildings; for the first time Ed caught sight of those whom he had come to consult.

"Is that the old woman?" he demanded, as a thin, withered shape appeared briefly at the top of the steps, glanced over the waiting people, and selected one. She conferred with a plump man, and then a muscular giant joined the discussion. "My God," Ed said, "is there an *organization* of them?"

"Different ones do different things," Barbara answered. Clutching the baby tight, she edged her way forward into the waiting mass of people. "We want to see the healer—we'll have to stand with that group over to the right, waiting by that tree."

Porter sat in the kitchen of the shelter, smoking and drinking coffee, his feet up on the windowsill, vaguely watching the shuffling line of people moving through the front door and into the various rooms.

"A lot of them, today," he said to Jack. "What we need is a flat cover-charge."

Jack grunted angrily and shook back his mane of blond hair. "Why aren't you out helping instead of sitting here guzzling coffee?"

"Nobody wants to peep into the future." Porter belched noisily; he was plump and flabby, blue-eyed, with thin damp hair. "When somebody wants to know if they're going to strike it rich or marry a beautiful woman I'll be there in my booth to advise them."

"Fortune-telling," Jack muttered. He stood restlessly by the window, great arms folded, face stern with worry. "That's what we're down to."

"I can't help that they ask me. One old geezer asked me when he was going to die; when I told him thirty-one days he turned red as a beet and started screaming at me. One thing, I'm honest. I tell them the truth, not what they want to hear." Porter grinned. "I'm not a quack."

"How long has it been since somebody asked you something important?"

"You mean something of abstract significance?" Porter lazily searched his mind. "Last week a fellow asked me if there'd ever be interplanetary ships again. I told him not that I could see."

"Did you also tell him you can't see worth a damn? A half year at the most?"

Porter's toad-like face bloomed contentedly. "He didn't ask me that."

The thin, withered old woman entered the kitchen briefly. "Lord," Thelma gasped, sinking down in a chair and pouring herself coffee. "I'm exhausted. And there must be fifty of them out there waiting to get healed." She examined her shaking hands. "Two bone cancers in one day about finishes me. I think the baby will survive, but the other's too far gone even for me. The baby will have to come back." Her voice trailed off wearily. "Back again next week."

"It'll be slower tomorrow," Porter predicted. "Ash storm down from Canada will keep most of them at their communes. Of course, after that—" He broke off and eyed Jack curiously. "What are you upset about? Everybody's growling around, today."

"I just came from Butterford," Jack answered moodily. "I'm going back later and try again."

Thelma shuddered. Porter looked away uneasily; he disliked hearing about conversations with a man whose bones were piled in the basement of the shelter. An almost superstitious fear drifted through the plump body of the precog. It was one thing to preview the future; seeing ahead was a positive, progressive talent. But returning to the past, to men already dead, to cities now turned to ash and rubble, places erased from the maps, participating in events long since forgotten—it was a sickly, neurotic rehashing of what had already been. Picking and stirring among the bones—literally bones—of the past.

"What did he say?" Thelma asked.

"The same as always," Jack answered.

"How many times is this?"

Jack's lips twisted. "Eleven times. And he knows it—I told him."

Thelma moved from the kitchen, out into the hall. "Back to work." She lingered at the door. "Eleven times and always the same. I've been making computations. How old are you, Jack?"

"How old do I look?"

"About thirty. You were born in 1946. This is 2017. That makes you seventy-one years old. I'd say I'm talking to an entity about a third of the way along. Where's your current entity?"

"You should be able to figure that. Back in '76."

"Doing what?"

Jack didn't answer. He knew perfectly well what his entity of this date, 2017, was doing back in the past. The old man of seventy-one years was lying in a medical hospital at one of the military centers, receiving treatment for a gradually worsening nephritis. He shot a quick glance at Porter to see if the precog was going to volunteer information previewed from the future. There was no expression on Porter's languid features, but that proved nothing. He'd have to get Stephen to probe into Porter if he really wanted to be sure.

Like the common workers who filed in daily to learn if they were going to strike it rich and marry happily, he wanted vitally to know the date of his own death. He *had* to know—it went beyond mere wanting.

He faced Porter squarely. "Let's have it. What do you see about me in the next six months?"

Porter yawned. "Am I supposed to orate the whole works? It'll take hours."

Jack relaxed, weak with relief. Then he would survive another six months, at least. In that he could bring to a successful completion his discussions with General Ernest Butterford, chief of staff of the armed forces of the United States. He pushed past Thelma and out of the kitchen.

"Where are you going?" she demanded.

"Back to see Butterford again. I'm going to make one more try."

"You always say that," Thelma complained peevishly.

"And I always am," Jack said. *Until I'm dead,* he thought bitterly, resentfully. Until the half conscious old man lying in the hospital bed at Baltimore, Maryland, passes away or is destroyed to make room for some wounded private carted by boxcar from the front lines, charged by Soviet napalm, crippled by nerve gas, insane from metallic ash-particles. When the ancient corpse was thrown out—and it wouldn't be long—there would be no more discussion with General Butterford.

First, he descended the stairs to the supply lockers in the basement of the shelter. Doris lay asleep on her bed in the corner, dark hair like cobwebs over her coffee-colored features, one bare arm raised, a heap of clothing strewn on the chair beside the bed. She awoke sleepily, stirred, and half sat up.

"What time is it?"

Jack glanced at his wristwatch. "One-thirty in the afternoon." He began opening one of the intricate locks that sealed in their supplies. Presently he slid a metal case down a rail and onto the cement floor. He swung an overhead light around and clicked it on.

The girl watched with interest. "What are you doing?" She tossed her covers back and got to her feet, stretched, and padded barefoot over to him. "I could have brought it out for you without all that work."

From the lead-lined case Jack removed the carefully stacked heap of bones and remnants of personal possessions: wallet, identification papers, photographs, fountain pen, bits of tattered uniform, a gold wedding ring, some silver coins. "He died under difficulties," Jack murmured. He examined the data-tape, made sure it was complete, and then slammed shut the case. "I told him I would bring this. Of course, he won't remember."

"Each time erases the last?" Doris wandered over to get her clothes. "It's really the same time again and again, isn't it?"

"The same interval," Jack admitted, "but there's no repetition of material."

Doris eyed him slyly as she struggled into her jeans. "*Some* repetition . . . it always comes out the same, no matter what you do. Butterford goes ahead and presents his recommendations to the President."

Jack didn't hear her. He had already moved back, taken his series of steps along the time-path. The basement, Doris' half-dressed figure, wavered and receded, as if seen through the bottom of a glass gradually filled with opaque liquid. Darkness, mixed with shifting textures of density, wavered around him as he walked sternly forward, the metal case gripped. *Backward,* actually. He was retreating along the direction in which the flow itself moved. Changing places with an earlier John Tremaine, the pimple-faced boy of sixteen who had trudged dutifully to high school, in the year 1962 A. D. in the city of Chicago, Illinois. This was a switch he had made many times. His younger entity should be resigned, by now . . . but he hoped idly that Doris would be finished dressing when the boy emerged.

The darkness that was no-time dwindled, and he blinked in a sudden torrent of yellow sunlight. Still gripping his metal case he made the final step backward and found himself in the center of a vast murmuring room. People drifted on all sides; several gaped at him, paralyzed with astonishment. For a moment he couldn't place the spatial location—and then memory came, a swift bitter flood of nostalgia.

He was back in the high school library where he had spent much time. The familiar place of books and bright-faced youths, gaily-dressed girls giggling and studying and flirting . . . young people totally oblivious of the approaching war. The mass death that would leave nothing of this city but dead, drifting ash.

He hurried from the library, conscious of the circle of bewilderment he had left behind. It was awkward to make a switch in which the passive entity was near other people; the abrupt transformation of a sixteen-year-old high school boy into the stern, towering figure of a thirty-year-old man was difficult to assimilate, even in a society theoretically aware of Psionic powers.

Theoretically—because at this date public consciousness was minimal. Awe and disbelief were the primary emotions; the surge of hopefulness hadn't begun. Psi-powers seemed miraculous only; the realization that these powers were at the disposal of the public wouldn't set in for a number of years.

He emerged on the busy Chicago street and hailed a taxi. The roar of buses, autos, the metallic swirl of buildings and people and signs, dazed him. Activity on all sides: the ordinary harmless routines of the common citizen, remote from the lethal planning at top levels. The people on all sides of him were about to be traded for the chimera of international prestige . . .

human life for metaphysical phantoms. He gave the cabdriver the address of Butterford's hotel suite and settled back to prepare himself for the familiar encounter.

The first steps were routine. He gave his identification to the battery of armed guards, was checked, searched, and processed into the suite. For fifteen minutes he sat in a luxurious anteroom smoking and restlessly waiting—as always. There were no alterations he could make here: the changes, if they were to materialize, came later.

"Do you know who I am?" he began bluntly, when the tiny, suspicious head of General Butterford was stuck from an inner office. He advanced grimly, case gripped. "This is the twelfth visit; there had better be results, this time."

Butterford's deep-set little eyes danced hostilely behind his thick glasses. "You're one of those supermen," he squeaked. "Those Psionics." He blocked the door with his wizened, uniformed body. "Well? What do you want? My time's valuable."

Jack seated himself facing the general's desk and corps of aides. "You have the analysis of my talent and history in your hands. You know what I can do."

Butterford glanced hostilely at the report. "You move into time. So?" His eyes narrowed. "What do you mean, *twelfth* time?" He grabbed up a heap of memoranda. "I've never seen you before. State what you have to say and then get out; I'm busy."

"I have a present for you," Jack said grimly. He carried the metal case to the desk, unsnapped it, and exposed the contents. "They belong to you—go ahead, take them out and run your hands over them."

Butterford gazed with revulsion at the bones. "What is this, some sort of anti-war exhibit? Are you Psis mixed up with those Jehovah's Witnesses?" His voice rose shrilly, resentfully. "Is this something you expect to pressure me with?"

"These are your goddamn bones!" Jack shouted in the man's face. He overturned the case; the contents spilled out on the desk and floor. "*Touch them!* You're going to die in this war, like everybody else. You're going to suffer and die hideously—they're going to get you with bacterial poisons one year and six days from this date. You'll live long enough to see the total destruction of organized society and then you'll go the way of everybody else!"

It would have been easier if Butterford were a coward. He sat gazing down at the tattered remains, the coins and pictures and rusting possessions, his face white, body stiff as metal. "I don't know whether to believe you," he said finally. "I never really believed any of this Psi-stuff."

"That's totally untrue," Jack answered hotly. "There isn't a government on the planet ignorant of us. You and the Soviet Union have been trying to organize us since '58, when we made ourselves known."

The discussion was on ground that Butterford understood. His eyes blazed furiously. "That's the whole point! If you Psis cooperated there wouldn't be those bones." He jabbed wildly at the pale heap on the desk. "You come here and blame me for the war. Blame yourselves—you won't put your shoulders to the wheel. How can we hope to come out of this war unless everybody does his part?" He leaned meaningfully toward Jack. "You came from the future, you say. Tell me what you Psis are going to do in the war. Tell me the part you're going to play."

"No part."

Butterford settled back triumphantly. "You're going to stand idly by?"

"Absolutely."

"And you came here to blame *me?*"

"If we help," Jack said carefully, "we help at policy level, not as hired servants. Otherwise, we will stand on the sidelines, waiting. We're available, but if winning the war depends on us, we want to say how that war will be won. Or whether there'll be a war at all." He slammed the metal case shut. "Otherwise, we might become apprehensive, as the scientists did in the middle fifties. We might begin to lose *our* enthusiasm . . . and also become bad security risks."

In Jack's mind a voice spoke, thin and bitter. A telepathic member of the Guild, a Psi of the present, monitoring the discussion from the New York office. "Very well-spoken. But you've lost. You lack the ability to maneuver him . . . all you've done is defend our position.

You haven't even brought up the possibility of changing his."

It was true. Desperately, Jack said: "I didn't come back here to state the Guild's position—you know our position! I came to lay the facts out in front of you. I came here from 2017. The war is over. Only a remnant survives. These are the facts, events that have taken place. You're going to recommend to the President that the United States call Russia's bluff on Java." His words came out individually, icily. "It's not a bluff. It means total war. Your recommendation is in error."

Butterford bristled. "You want us to back down? Let them take over the free world?"

Twelve times: impasse. He had accomplished nothing. "You'd go into the war knowing you can't win?"

"We'll fight," Butterford said. "Better an honorable war than a dishonorable peace."

"No war is honorable. War means death, barbarism, and mass destruction."

"What does peace mean?"

"Peace means the growth of the Guild. In fifty years our presence will shift the ideology of both blocs. We're above the war; we straddle both worlds. There're Psis here and in Russia; we're part of no country. The scientists could have been that, once. But they chose to cooperate with national governments. Now it's up to us."

Butterford shook his head. "No," he said firmly. "You're not going to influence us. *We* make policy . . . if you act, you act in line with our directives. Or you don't act. You stay out."

"We'll stay out."

Butterford leaped up. "*Traitors!*" he shouted as Jack left the office. "You don't have a choice! We demand your abilities! We'll hunt you out and grab you one by one. You've got to cooperate—everybody's got to cooperate. This is total war!"

The door closed, and he was in the anteroom.

"No, there isn't any hope," the voice in his mind stated bleakly. "I can prove that you've done this twelve times. And you're contemplating a thirteenth. Give up. The withdrawal order has been given out already. When the war begins we'll be aloof."

"We ought to help!" Jack said futilely. "Not the war—we ought to help *them,* the people who're going to be killed by the millions."

"We can't. We're not gods. We're only humans with paratalents. We can help, if they accept us, allow us to help. We can't force our views on them. We can't force the Guild in, if the governments don't want us."

Gripping the metal case, Jack headed numbly down the stairs, toward the street. Back to the high school library.

At the dinner table, with black night lying outside the shelter, he faced the other surviving Guild members. "So here we are. Outside society—doing nothing. Not harming and not helping. *Useless!*" He smashed his fist convulsively against the rotting wooden wall. "Peripheral and useless, and while we sit here the communes fall apart and what's left collapses."

Thelma spooned up her soup impassively. "We heal the sick, read the future, offer advice, and perform miracles."

"We've been doing that thousands of years," Jack answered bitterly. "Sibyls, witches, perched on deserted hills outside towns. *Can't we get in and help?* Do we always have to be on the outside, we who understand what's going on? Watching the blind fools lead mankind to destruction! Couldn't we have stopped the war, forced peace on them?"

Porter said languidly, "We don't want to force anything on them, Jack. You know that. We're not their masters. We want to help them, not control them."

The meal continued in gloomy silence. Doris said presently, "The trouble is with the governments. It's the politicians who're jealous of us." She smiled mournfully across the table at Jack. "They know if we had our way, a time would come when politicians wouldn't be needed."

Thelma attacked her plate of dried beans and broiled rabbit in a thin paste of gravy. "There isn't much of a government, these days. It isn't like it was before the war. You can't really call a few majors sitting around in commune offices a *government.*"

"They make the decisions," Porter pointed out. "They decided what commune policy will be."

"I know of a commune up north," Stephen said, "in

which the workers killed the officers and took over. They're dying out. It won't be long before they're extinct."

Jack pushed his plate away and got to his feet. "I'm going out on the porch." He left the kitchen, crossed through the deserted living room and opened the steel-reinforced front door. Cold evening wind swirled around him as he blindly felt his way to the railing and stopped, hands in his pockets, gazing sightlessly out at the vacant field.

The rusty fleet of cars was gone. Nothing stirred except the withered trees along the road, dry rustles in the restless night wind. A dismal sight; overhead a few stars glowed fitfully. Far off somewhere an animal crashed after its prey, a wild dog or perhaps a quasi-human living down in the ruined cellars of Chicago.

After a time Doris appeared behind him. Silently, she came up and stood next to him, a slim dark shape in the night gloom, her arms folded against the cold. "You're not going to try again?" she asked softly.

"Twelve is enough. I—can't change him. I don't have the ability. I'm not adroit enough." Jack spread his massive hands miserably. "He's a clever little chicken of a thing. Like Thelma—scrawny and full of talk. Again and again I get back there—and what can I do?"

Doris touched his arm wistfully. "How does it look? I never saw cities full of life, before the war. Remember, I was born in a military camp."

"You'd like it. People laughing and hurrying. Cars, signs, life everywhere. It drives me crazy. I wish I couldn't see it—to be able to step from here to there." He indicated the twisted trees. "Ten steps back from those trees, and there it is. And yet it's gone forever . . . even for me. There'll be a time when I can't step there either, like the rest of you."

Doris failed to understand him. "Isn't it strange?" she murmured. "I can move anything in the world, but I can't move myself back, the way you do." She made a slight flutter of her hands; in the darkness something slapped against the rail of the porch and she bent over to retrieve it. "See the pretty bird? Stunned, not dead." She tossed the bird up and it managed to struggle off into the shrubs. "I've got so I only stun them."

Jack wasn't pleased. "That's what we do with our talents. Tricks, games. Nothing more."

"That isn't so!" Doris objected. "Today when I got up, there was a bunch of doubters. Stephen caught their thoughts and sent me out." Pride tingled in her voice. "I brought an underground spring up to the surface—it burst out everywhere and got them all soaked, before I sent it back. They were convinced."

"Did it ever occur to you," Jack said, "that you could make it possible for them to rebuild their cities?"

"They don't want to rebuild cities."

"They don't think they can. They've given up the idea of rebuilding. It's a lost concept." He brooded unhappily. "There's too many millions of miles of ruined ash, and too few people. They don't even try to unify the communes."

"They have radios," Doris pointed out. "They can talk to each other, if they want."

"If they use them, the war will start up again. They know there're pockets of fanatics left who'd be happy to start the war, given half the chance. They'd rather sink into barbarism than get that started." He spat into the weedy bushes growing beneath the porch. "I don't blame them."

"If we controlled the communes," Doris said thoughtfully, "we wouldn't start up the war. We'd unify them on a peaceful basis."

"You're playing all sides at once," Jack said angrily. "A minute ago you were performing miracles—where'd this thought come from?"

Doris hesitated. "Well, I was just passing it on. I guess Stephen really said it, or thought it. I just spoke it out loud."

"You enjoy being a mouthpiece for Stephen?"

Doris fluttered fearfully. "My God, Jack—he can probe you. Don't say things like that!"

Jack stepped away from her and down the porch steps. He rapidly crossed the dark, silent field, away from the shelter. The girl hurried after him.

"Don't walk off," she gasped breathlessly. "Stephen's just a kid. He's not like you, grown-up and big. Mature."

Jack laughed upward at the black sky. "You damn fool. Do you know how old I am?"

"No," Doris said, "and don't say. I know you're older than I am. You've always been around; I remember you when I was just a kid. You were always big and strong and blond." She giggled nervously. "Of course, all those *others* . . . those different persons, old and young. I don't really understand, but they're all you, I guess. Different yous along your time-path."

"That's right," Jack said tightly. "They're all me."

"That one today, when you switched down in the basement, when I was sleeping." Doris caught his arm and tucked her cold fingers around his wrist. "Just a kid, with books under his arm, in a green sweater and brown slacks."

"Sixteen years old," Jack muttered.

"He was cute. Shy, flustered. Younger than I am. We went upstairs and he watched the crowd; that was when Stephen called me to do the miracle. He—I mean, *you*—stood around so interested. Porter kidded him. Porter doesn't mean any harm—he likes to eat and sleep and that's about all. He's all right. Stephen kidded him, too. I don't think Stephen liked him."

"You mean he doesn't like me."

"I—guess you know how we feel. All of us, to some degree . . . we wonder why you keep going back again and again, trying to patch up the past. The past is over! Maybe not to you . . . but it really is over. You can't change it; the war came, this is all ruined, only remnants are left. You said it yourself: *why are we on the outside?* We could so easily be on the inside." Childish excitement thrilled through her; she pushed against him eagerly, carried away by her flow of words. "Forget the past—let's work with the present! The material is here; the people, the objects. Let's move it all around. Pick it up, set it down." She lifted a grove of trees a mile away; the whole top of a line of hills burst loose, rose high in the air, and then disslved in booming fragments. "We can take things apart and put them back together!"

"I'm seventy-one years old," Jack said. "There isn't going to be any putting together for me. And I'm through picking over the past. I'm not going to try anymore. You can all rejoice . . . I'm finished."

She tugged at him fiercely. "Then it's up to the rest of us!"

If he had Porter's talent he could see beyond his death. Porter would, at some future time, view his own corpse stretched out, view his burial, continue to live month after month, while his plump corpse rotted underground. Porter's bovine contentedness was possible in a man who could preview the future. . . . Jack twisted wretchedly as anguished uncertainty ached through him. After the dying old man in the military hospital reached the inevitable end of his life-span—what then? What happened *here*, among the survivors of the Guild?

Beside him, the girl babbled on. The possibilities he had suggested: real material to work with, not tricks or miracles. For her, the possibilities of social action were swimming into existence. They were all restless, except perhaps Porter. Tired of standing idle. Impatient with the anachronistic officers who kept the communes alive, misguided remnants of a past order of incompetents who had proved their unfitness to rule by leading their block to almost total destruction.

Rule by the Guild couldn't be worse.

Or could it? Something had survived rule by power-oriented politicians, professional spellbinders recruited from smoke-dingy city halls and cheap law offices. If Psionic rule failed, if analogues of the struggle of national states arose, there might be nothing spared. The collective power of the Guild reached into all dimensions of life; for the first time a genuine totalitarian society could arise. Dominated by telepaths, precogs, healers with the power to animate inorganic matter and to wither organic matter, what ordinary person could survive?

There would be no recourse against the Guild. Man controlled by Psionic organizers would be powerless. It was merely a question of time before the maintenance of non-Psis would be seriously scrutinized, with an eye toward greater efficiency, toward the elimination of useless material. Rule by supercompetents could be worse than rule by incompetents.

"Worse for whom?" Stephen's clear, treble thoughts came into his mind. Cold, confident, utterly without doubt. "You can see they're dying out. It's not a question of our eliminating them; it's a question of how long are we going to maintain their artificial preservation? We're running a zoo, Jack. We're keeping alive an extinct species. And the cage is too large . . . it takes up all the world. Give them some space, if you want. A subcontinent. But we deserve the balance for our own use."

Porter sat scooping up baked rice pudding from his dish. He continued eating even after Stephen began screaming. It wasn't until Thelma clawed his hand loose from his spoon that he gave up and turned his attention to what was happening.

Surprise was totally unknown to him; six months earlier he had examined the scene, reflected on it, and turned his attention to later events. Reluctantly, he pushed back his chair and dragged his heavy body upright.

"He's going to kill me!" Stephen was wailing. "Why didn't you tell me?" he shouted at Porter. "You knew—he's coming to kill me right now."

"For God's sake," Thelma shrilled in Porter's ear, "is it true? Can't you do something? You're a man—stop him!"

While Porter gathered a reply, Jack entered the kitchen. Stephen's shrill wails grew frantic. Doris hurried wild-eyed after Jack, her talent forgotten in the abrupt explosion of excitement. Thelma hurried around the table, between Jack and the boy, scrawny arms out, dried-up face contorted with outrage.

"I can see it!" Stephen screamed. "In his mind—he's going to kill me because he knows I want to—" He broke off. "He doesn't want us to do anything. He wants us to stay here in this old ruin, doing tricks for people." Fury broke through his terror. "I'm not going to do it. I'm through doing mind-reading tricks. Now he's thinking about killing all of us! He wants us all dead!"

Porter settled down in his chair and pawed for his spoon. He pulled his plate under his chin; eyes intently on Jack and Stephen, he continued slowly eating.

"I'm sorry," Jack said. "You shouldn't have told me your thoughts, I couldn't have read them. You could have kept them to yourself." He moved forward.

Thelma grabbed him with her skinny claws and hung on tight. The wail and babble rose in hysteria; Porter winced and bobbed his thick neck-wattles. Impassively, he watched Jack and the old woman struggle together; beyond them, Stephen stood paralyzed with childish terror, face waxen, youthful body rigid.

Doris moved forward, and Porter stopped eating. A kind of tension settled over him; but it was a finality that made him forget eating, not doubt or uncertainty. Knowing what was going to happen didn't diminish the awesomeness of it. He couldn't be surprised . . . but he could be sobered.

"Leave him alone," Doris gasped. "He's just a boy. Go sit down and behave yourself." She caught hold of Jack around the waist; the two women swayed back and forth, trying to hold the immense muscular figure. "Stop it! Leave him alone!"

Jack broke away. He tottered, tried to regain his balance. The two women fluttered and clawed after him like furious birds; he reached back to push them away. . . .

"Don't look," Porter said sharply.

Doris turned in his direction. And didn't see, as he anticipated. Thelma saw, and her voice suddenly died into silence. Stephen choked off, horrified, then screeched in stricken dismay.

They had seen the last entity along Jack's time-path once before. Briefly one night the withered old man had appeared, as the more youthful entity inspected the military hospital to analyze its resources. The younger Jack had returned at once, satisfied that the dying old man would be given the best treatment available. In that moment they had seen his gaunt, fever-ridden face. This time the eyes weren't bright. Lusterless, the eyes of a dead object gazed blankly at them, as the hunched figure remained briefly upright.

Thelma tried vainly to catch it as it pitched forward. Like a sack of meal it crashed into the table, scattering cups and silver. It wore a faded blue robe, knotted at the waist. Its pale-white feet were bare. From it oozed the pungent hygienic scent of the hospital, of age and illness and death.

"You did it," Porter said. "Both of you together. Doris, especially. But it would have come in the next few days, anyhow." He added, "Jack's dead. We'll have to bury him, unless you think any of you can bring him back."

Thelma stood wiping at her eyes. Tears dribbled down her shrunken cheeks, into her mouth. "It was my fault. I wanted to destroy him. My hands." She held up her claws. "He never trusted me; he never put himself in my care. And he was right."

"We both did it," Doris muttered, shaken. "Porter's telling the truth. I wanted him to go away . . . I wanted him to leave. I never moved anything into time, before."

"You never will again," Porter said. "He left no descendants. He was the first and the last man to move through time. It was a unique talent."

Stephen was recovering slowly, still white-faced and shaken, eyes fixed on the withered shape in its frayed blue pajamas, spread out under the table. "Anyhow," he muttered finally, "there won't be any more picking over the past."

"I believe," Thelma said tightly, "you can follow my thoughts. Are you aware of what I'm thinking?"

Stephen blinked. "Yes."

"Now listen carefully. I'm going to put them into words so everybody will hear them."

Stephen nodded without speaking. His eyes darted frantically around the room, but he didn't stir.

"There are now four Guild members," Thelma said. Her voice was flat and low, without expression. "Some of us want to leave this place and enter the communes. Some of us think this would be a good time to impose ourselves on the communes, whether they like it or not."

Stephen nodded.

"I would say," Thelma continued, examining her ancient, dried-up hands, "that if any of us tries to leave here, I will do what Jack tried to do." She pondered. "But I don't know if I can. Maybe I'll fail, too."

"Yes," Stephen said. His voice trembled, then gained strength. "You're not strong enough. There's somebody here a lot stronger than you. She can pick you up and put you down anywhere she wants. On the other side of the world—on the moon—in the middle of the ocean."

Doris made a faint strangled sound. "I—"

"That's true," Thelma agreed. "But I'm standing only

three feet from her. If I touch her first she'll be drained." She studied the smooth, frightened face of the girl. "But you're right. What happens depends not on you or me, but on what Doris wants to do."

Doris breathed rapidly, huskily. "I don't know," she said, faintly. "I don't want to stay here, just sitting around in this old ruin, day after day, doing—tricks. But Jack always said we shouldn't force ourselves on the communes." Her voice trailed off uncertainly. "All my life, as long as I can remember, when I was a little girl growing up, there was Jack saying over and over again we shouldn't force them. If they didn't want us . . ."

"She won't move you now," Stephen said to Thelma, "but she will eventually. Sooner or later she'll move you away from here, some night when you're sleeping. Eventually she'll make up her mind." He grinned starkly. "Remember, I can talk to her, silently in her mind. Any time I want."

"Will you?" Thelma asked the girl.

Doris faltered miserably. "I—don't know. *Will I?* . . . Maybe so. It's so—bewildering."

Porter sat up straight in his chair, leaned back, and belched loudly. "It's strange to hear you all conjecturing," he said. "As a matter of fact, you won't touch Thelma." To the old woman he said, "There's nothing to worry about. I can see this stalemate going on. The four of us balance each other—we'll stay where we are."

Thelma sagged. "Maybe Stephen's right. If we have to keep on living this way, doing nothing—"

"We'll be here," Porter said, "but we won't be living the way we've been living."

"What do you mean?" Thelma demanded. "How will we be living? *What's going to happen?"*

"It's hard to probe you," Stephen said to Porter peevishly. "These are things you've seen, not things you're thinking. Have the commune governments changed their position? Are they finally going to call us in?"

"The governments won't call us in," Porter said. "We'll never be invited into the communes, any more than we were invited into Washington and Moscow. We've had to stand outside waiting." He glanced up and stated enigmatically, "That waiting is about over."

It was early morning. Ed Garby brought the rumbling, battered truck into line behind the other surface cars leaving the commune. Cold, fitful sunlight filtered down on the concrete squares that made up the commune installations; today was going to be another cloudy day, exactly like the last. Even so, the exit check-gate ahead was already clogged with outgoing traffic.

"A lot of them, this morning," his wife murmured. "I guess they can't wait any longer for the ash to lift."

Ed clutched for his pass, buried in his sweat-gummed shirt pocket. "The gate's a bottleneck," he muttered resentfully. "What are they doing, getting into the cars?"

There were four guards, today, not the usual one. A squad of armed troops that moved back and forth among the stalled cars, peering and murmuring, reporting through their neck-mikes to the commune offices below surface. A massive truck loaded with workers pulled suddenly away from the line and onto a side road. Roaring and belching clouds of foul blue gas, it made a complete circle and lumbered back toward the center of the commune, away from the exit gate. Ed watched it uneasily.

"What's it doing, turning back?" Fear clutched him. "They're turning us back!"

"No, they're not," Barbara said quietly. "Look—there goes a car through."

An ancient wartime pleasure car precariously edged through the gate and out onto the plain beyond the commune. A second followed it and the two cars gathered speed to climb the long low ridge that became the first tangle of trees.

A horn honked behind Ed. Convulsively, he moved the car forward. In Barbara's lap the baby wailed anxiously; she wound its seedy cotton blanket around it and rolled up the window. "It's an awful day. If we didn't have to go—" She broke off. "Here come the guards. Get the pass out."

Ed greeted the guards apprehensively. "Morning."

Curtly, one of the guards took his pass, examined it, punched it, and filed it away in a steel-bound notebook. "Each of you prepare your thumb for prints," he instructed. A black, oozing pad was passed up. "Including the baby."

Ed was astounded. "Why? What the hell's going on?"

The twins were too terrified to move. Numbly, they allowed the guards to take their prints. Ed protested weakly, as the pad was pushed against his thumb. His wrist was grabbed and yanked forward. As the guards walked around the truck to get at Barbara, the squad leader placed his boot on the running board and addressed Ed briefly.

"Five of you. Family?"

Ed nodded mutely. "Yeah, my family."

"Complete? Any more?"

"No. Just us five."

The guard's dark eyes bored down at him. "When are you coming back?"

"Tonight." Ed indicated the metal notebook in which his pass had been filed. "It says, before six."

"If you go through that gate," the guard said, "you won't be coming back. That gate only goes one way."

"Since when?" Barbara whispered, face ashen.

"Since last night. It's your choice. Go ahead out there, get your business done, consult your soothsayer. But don't come back." The guard pointed to the side road. "If you want to turn around, that road takes you to the descent ramps. Follow the truck ahead—it's turning back."

Ed licked his dry lips. "I can't. My kid—she's got bone cancer. The old woman started her healing, but she isn't well, not yet. The old woman says today she can finish."

The guard examined a dog-eared directory. "Ward 9, sixth level. Go down there and they'll fix up your kid. The docs have all the equipment." He closed the book and stepped back from the car, a heavy-set man, red-faced, with bristled, beefy skin. "Let's get started, buddy. One way or the other. It's your choice."

Automatically, Ed moved the car forward. "They must have decided," he muttered, dazed. "Too many people going out. They want to scare us . . . they know we can't live out there. We'd die out there!"

Barbara quietly clutched the baby. "We'll die here eventually."

"But it's nothing but ruins out there!"

"Aren't *they* out there?"

Ed choked helplessly. "We can't come back—suppose it's a mistake?"

The truck ahead wavered toward the side road. An uncertain hand signal was made; suddenly the driver yanked his hand in and wobbled the truck back toward the exit gate. A moment of confusion took place. The truck slowed almost to a stop; Ed slammed on his brakes, cursed, and shifted into low. Then the truck ahead gained speed. It rumbled through the gate and out onto the barren ground. Without thinking, Ed followed it. Cold, ash-heavy air swept into the cabin as he gained speed and pulled up beside the truck. Even with it he leaned out and shouted, "Where you going? They won't let you back!"

The driver, a skinny little man, bald and bony, shouted angrily back, "Goddamn it, I'm not coming back! The hell with them—I got all my food and bedding in here—I got every damn thing I own. Let them try to get me back!" He gunned up his truck and pulled ahead of Ed.

"Well," Barbara said quietly, "it's done. We're outside."

"Yeah," Ed agreed shakily. "We are. A yard, a thousand miles—it's all the same." In panic, he turned wildly to his wife. "What if they don't take us? I mean, what if we get there and they don't want us. All they got is that old broken-down wartime shelter. There isn't room for anybody—and look behind us."

A line of hesitant, lumbering trucks and cars was picking its way uncertainly from the gate, streaming rustily out onto the parched plain. A few pulled out and swung back; one pulled over to the side of the road and halted while its passengers argued with bitter desperation.

"They'll take us," Barbara said. "They want to help us—they always wanted to."

"But suppose they *can't!*"

"I think they can. There's a lot of power there, if we ask for it. They couldn't come to us, but we can go to them. We've been held back too long, separated from them too many years. If the government won't let them in, then we'll have to go outside."

"Can we live outside?" Ed asked hoarsely.

"Yes."

Behind them a horn honked excitedly. Ed gained speed. "It's a regular exodus. Look at them pouring out. Who'll be left?"

"There'll be plenty left," Barbara answered. "All the big shots will stay behind." She laughed breathlessly. "Maybe they'll be able to get the war going again. It'll give them something to do, while we're away."

THE COMMUTER

THE little fellow was tired. He pushed his way slowly through the throng of people, across the lobby of the station, to the ticket window. He waited his turn impatiently, fatigue showing in his drooping shoulders, his sagging brown coat.

"Next," Ed Jacobson, the ticket seller, rasped.

The little fellow tossed a five dollar bill on the counter. "Give me a new commute book. Used up the old one." He peered past Jacobson at the wall clock. "Lord, is it really that late?"

Jacobson accepted the five dollars. "OK, mister. One commute book. Where to?"

"Macon Heights," the little fellow stated.

"Macon Heights." Jacobson consulted his board. "Macon Heights. There isn't any such place."

The little man's face hardened in suspicion. "You trying to be funny?"

"Mister, there isn't any Macon Heights. I can't sell you a ticket unless there is such a place."

"What do you mean? I live there!"

"I don't care. I've been selling tickets for six years and there is no such place."

The little man's eyes popped with astonishment. "But I have a home there. I go there every night. I—"

"Here." Jacobson pushed him his chart board. "You find it."

The little man pulled the board over to one side. He studied it frantically, his finger trembling as he went down the list of towns.

"Find it?" Jacobson demanded, resting his arms on the counter. "It's not there, is it?"

The little man shook his head, dazed. "I don't understand. It doesn't make sense. Something must be wrong. There certainly must be some—"

Suddenly he vanished. The board fell to the cement floor. The little fellow was gone—winked out of existence.

"Holy Caesar's Ghost," Jacobson gasped. His mouth opened and closed. There was only the board lying on the cement floor.

The little man had ceased to exist.

"What then?" Bob Paine asked.

"I went around and picked up the board."

"He was really gone?"

"He was gone, all right." Jacobson mopped his forehead. "I wish you had been around. Like a light he went out. Completely. No sound. No motion."

Paine lit a cigarette, leaning back in his chair. "Had you ever seen him before?"

"No."

"What time of day was it?"

"Just about now. About five." Jacobson moved toward the ticket window. "Here comes a bunch of people."

"Macon Heights." Paine turned the pages of the State city guide. "No listing in any of the books. If he reappears I want to talk to him. Get him inside the office."

"Sure. I don't want to have nothing to do with him. It isn't natural." Jacobson turned to the window. "Yes, lady."

"Two round trip tickets to Lewisburg."

Paine stubbed his cigarette out and lit another. "I keep feeling I've heard the name before." He got up and wandered over to the wall map. "But it isn't listed."

"There is no listing because there is no such place," Jacobson said. "You think I could stand here daily, selling one ticket after another, and not know?" He turned back to his window. "Yes, sir."

"I'd like a commute book to Macon Heights," the little fellow said, glancing nervously at the clock on the wall. "And hurry it up."

Jacobson closed his eyes. He hung on tight. When he opened his eyes again the little fellow was still there. Small wrinkled face. Thinning hair. Glasses. Tired, slumped coat.

Jacobson turned and moved across the office to Paine. "He's back." Jacobson swallowed, his face pale. "It's him again."

Paine's eyes flickered. "Bring him right in."

Jacobson nodded and returned to his window. "Mister," he said, "could you please come inside?" He indicated the door. "The Vice-President would like to see you for a moment."

The little man's face darkened. "What's up? The train's about to take off." Grumbling under his breath, he pushed the door open and entered the office. "This sort of thing has never happened before. It's certainly getting hard to purchase a commute book. If I miss the train I'm going to hold your company—"

"Sit down," Paine said, indicating the chair across from his desk. "You're the gentleman who wants a commute book to Macon Heights?"

"Is there something strange about that? What's the matter with all of you? Why can't you sell me a commute book like you always do?"

"Like—like we *always* do?"

The little man held himself in check with great effort. "Last December my wife and I moved out to Macon Heights. I've been riding your train ten times a week, twice a day, for six months. Every month I buy a new commute book."

Paine leaned toward him. "Exactly which one of our trains do you take, Mr.—"

"Critchet. Ernest Critchet. The B train. Don't you know your own schedules?"

"The B train?" Paine consulted a B train chart, running his pencil along it. No Macon Heights was listed. "How long is the trip? How long does it take?"

"Exactly forty-nine minutes." Critchet looked up at the wall clock. "If I ever get on it."

Paine calculated mentally. Forty-nine minutes. About thirty miles from the city. He got up and crossed to the big wall map.

"What's wrong?" Critchet asked with marked suspicion.

Paine drew a thirty-mile circle on the map. The circle

crossed a number of towns, but none of them was Macon Heights. And on the B line there was nothing at all.

"What sort of place is Macon Heights?" Paine asked. "How many people, would you say?"

"I don't know. Five thousand, maybe. I spend most of my time in the city. I'm a bookkeeper over at Bradshaw Insurance."

"Is Macon Heights a fairly new place?"

"It's modern enough. We have a little two-bedroom house, a couple years old." Critchet stirred restlessly. "How about my commute book?"

"I'm afraid," Paine said slowly, "I can't sell you a commute book."

"What? Why not?"

"We don't have any service to Macon Heights."

Critchet leaped up. "What do you mean?"

"There's no such place. Look at the map yourself."

Critched gaped, his face working. Then he turned angrily to the wall map, glaring at it intently.

"This is a curious situation, Mr. Critchet," Paine murmured. "It isn't on the map, and the State city directory doesn't list it. We have no schedule that includes it. There are no commute books made up for it. We don't—"

He broke off. Critchet had vanished. One moment he was there, studying the wall map. The next moment he was gone. Vanished. Puffed out.

"Jacobson!" Paine barked. "He's gone!"

Jacobson's eyes grew large. Sweat stood out on his forehead. "So he is," he murmured.

Paine was deep in thought, gazing at the empty spot Ernest Critchet had occupied. "Something's going on," he muttered. "Something damn strange." Abruptly he grabbed his overcoat and headed for the door.

"Don't leave me alone!" Jacobson begged.

"If you need me I'll be at Laura's apartment. The number's some place in my desk."

"This is no time for games with girls."

Paine pushed open the door to the lobby. "I doubt," he said grimly, "if this is a game."

Paine climbed the stairs to Laura Nichols' apartment two at a time. He leaned on the buzzer until the door opened.

"Bob!" Laura blinked in surprise. "To what do I owe this—"

Paine pushed past her, inside the apartment. "Hope I'm not interrupting anything."

"No, but—"

"Big doings. I'm going to need some help. Can I count on you?"

"On me?" Laura closed the door after him. Her attractively furnished apartment lay in half shadow. At the end of the deep green couch a single table lamp burned. The heavy drapes were pulled. The phonograph was on low in the corner.

"Maybe I'm going crazy." Paine threw himself down on the luxuriant green couch. "That's what I want to find out."

"How can I help?" Laura came languidly over, her arms folded, a cigarette between her lips. She shook her long hair back out of her eyes. "Just what did you have in mind?"

Paine grinned at the girl appreciatively. "You'll be surprised. I want you to go downtown tomorrow morning bright and early and—"

"Tomorrow morning! I have a job, remember? And the office starts a whole new string of reports this week."

"The hell with that. Take the morning off. Go downtown to the main library. If you can't get the information there, go over to the county courthouse and start looking through the back tax records. Keep looking until you find it."

"It? Find what?"

Paine lit a cigarette thoughtfully. "Mention of a place called Macon Heights. I know I've heard the name before. Years ago. Got the picture? Go through the old atlases. Old newspapers in the reading room. Old magazines. Reports. City proposals. Propositions before the State legislature."

Laura sat down slowly on the arm of the couch. "Are you kidding?"

"No."

"How far back?"

"Maybe ten years—if necessary."

"Good Lord! I might have to—"

"Stay there until you find it." Paine got up abruptly. "I'll see you later."

"You're leaving? You're not taking me out to dinner?"

"Sorry." Paine moved toward the door. "I'll be busy. Real busy."

"Doing what?"

"Visiting Macon Heights."

Outside the train endless fields stretched off, broken by an occasional farm building. Bleak telephone poles jutted up toward the evening sky.

Paine glanced at his wristwatch. Not far, now. The train passed through a small town. A couple of gas stations, roadside stands, television store. It stopped at the station, brakes grinding. Lewisburg. A few commuters got off, men in overcoats with evening papers. The doors slammed and the train started up.

Paine settled back against his seat, deep in thought. Critchet had vanished while looking at the wall map. He had vanished the first time when Jacobson showed him the chart board.... When he had been shown there was no such place as Macon Heights. Was there some sort of clue there? The whole thing was unreal, dreamlike.

Paine peered out. He was almost there—if there were such a place. Outside the train the brown fields stretched off endlessly. Hills and level fields. Telephone poles. Cars racing along the State highway, tiny black specks hurrying through the twilight.

But no sign of Macon Heights.

The train roared on its way. Paine consulted his watch. Fifty-one minutes had passed. And he had seen nothing. Nothing but fields.

He walked up the car and sat down beside the conductor, a white-haired old gentleman. "Ever heard of a place called Macon Heights?" Paine asked.

"No, sir."

Paine showed his identification. "You're sure you never heard of any place by that name?"

"Positive, Mr. Paine."

"How long have you been on this run?"

"Eleven years, Mr. Paine."

Paine rode on until the next stop, Jacksonville. He got off and transferred to a B train heading back to the city. The sun had set. The sky was almost black. Dimly, he could make out the scenery out there beyond the window.

He tensed, holding his breath. One minute to go. Forty seconds. Was there anything? Level fields. Bleak telephone poles. A barren, wasted landscape between towns.

Between? The train rushed on, hurtling through the gloom. Paine gazed out fixedly. Was there something out there? Something beside the fields?

Above the fields a long mass of translucent smoke lay stretched out. A homogeneous mass, extended for almost a mile. What was it? Smoke from the engine? But the engine was diesel. From a truck along the highway? A brush fire? None of the fields looked burned.

Suddenly the train began to slow. Paine was instantly alert. The train was stopping, coming to a halt. The brakes screeched, the cars lurched from side to side. Then silence.

Across the aisle a tall man in a light coat got to his feet, put his hat on, and moved rapidly toward the door. He leaped down from the train, onto the ground. Paine watched him, fascinated. The man walked rapidly away from the train across the dark fields. He moved with purpose, heading toward the bank of gray haze.

The man rose. He was walking a foot off the ground. He turned to the right. He rose again, now—three feet off the ground. For a moment he walked parallel to the ground, still heading away from the train. Then he vanished into the bank of haze. He was gone.

Paine hurried up the aisle. But already the train had begun gathering speed. The ground moved past outside. Paine located the conductor, leaning against the wall of the car, a pudding-faced youth.

"Listen," Paine grated. "What was that stop!"

"Beg pardon, sir?"

"That stop! Where the hell were we?"

"We always stop there." Slowly, the conductor reached into his coat and brought out a handful of schedules. He sorted through them and passed one to Paine. "The B always stops at Macon Heights. Didn't you know that?"

"No!"

"It's on the schedule." The youth raised his pulp magazine again. "Always stops there. Always has. Always will."

Paine tore the schedule open. It was true. Macon Heights was listed between Jacksonville and Lewisburg. Exactly thirty miles from the city.

The cloud of gray haze. The vast cloud, gaining form rapidly. As if something were coming into existence. As a matter of fact, something *was* coming into existence.

Macon Heights!

He caught Laura at her apartment the next morning. She was sitting at the coffee table in a pale pink sweater and dark slacks. Before her was a pile of notes, a pencil and eraser, and a malted milk.

"How did you make out?" Paine demanded.

"Fine. I got your information."

"What's the story?"

"There was quite a bit of material." She patted the sheaf of notes. "I summed up the major parts for you."

"Let's have the summation."

"Seven years ago this August the county board of supervisors voted on three new suburban housing tracts to be set up outside the city. Macon Heights was one of them. There was a big debate. Most of the city merchants opposed the new tracts. Said they would draw too much retail business away from the city."

"Go on."

"There was a long fight. Finally two of the three tracts were approved. Waterville and Cedar Groves. But not Macon Heights."

"I see," Paine murmured thoughtfully.

"Macon Heights was defeated. A compromise; two tracts instead of three. The two tracts were built up right away. You know. We passed through Waterville one afternoon. Nice little place."

"But no Macon Heights."

"No. Macon Heights was given up."

Paine rubbed his jaw. "That's the story, then."

"That's the story. Do you realize I lose a whole half-day's pay because of this? You *have* to take me out, tonight. Maybe I should get another fellow. I'm beginning to think you're not such a good bet."

Paine nodded absently. "Seven years ago." All at once a thought came to him. "The vote! How close was the vote on Macon Heights?"

Laura consulted her notes. "The project was defeated by a single vote."

"A single vote. Seven years ago." Paine moved out into the hall. "Thanks, honey. Things are beginning to make sense. Lots of sense!"

He caught a cab out front. The cab raced him across the city, toward the train station. Outside, signs and streets flashed by. People and stores and cars.

His hunch had been correct. He *had* heard the name before. Seven years ago. A bitter county debate on a proposed suburban tract. Two towns approved; one defeated and forgotten.

But now the forgotten town was coming into existence—seven years later. The town and an undetermined slice of reality along with it. *Why?* Had something changed in the past? Had an alteration occurred in some past continuum?

That seemed like the explanation. The vote had been close. Macon Heights had *almost* been approved. Maybe certain parts of the past were unstable. Maybe that particular period, seven years ago, had been critical. Maybe it had never completely "jelled." An odd thought: the past changing, after it had already happened.

Suddenly Paine's eyes focused. He sat up quickly. Across the street was a store sign, halfway along the block. Over a small, inconspicuous establishment. As the cab moved forward Paine peered to see.

BRADSHAW INSURANCE
[OR]
NOTARY PUBLIC

He pondered. Critchet's place of business. Did it also come and go? Had it always been there? Something about it made him uneasy.

"Hurry it up," Paine ordered the driver. "Let's get going."

When the train slowed down at Macon Heights, Paine got quickly to his feet and made his way up the aisle to the door. The grinding wheels jerked to a halt and Paine leaped down onto the hot gravel siding. He looked around him.

In the afternoon sunlight, Macon Heights glittered and sparkled, its even rows of houses stretching out in all directions. In the center of the town the marquee of a theater rose up.

A theater, even. Paine headed across the track toward the town. Beyond the train station was a parking lot. He stepped up onto the lot and crossed it, following a path past a filling station and onto a sidewalk.

He came out on the main street of the town. A double row of stores stretched out ahead of him. A hardware store. Two drugstores. A dime store. A modern department store.

Paine walked along, hands in his pockets, gazing around him at Macon Heights. An apartment building stuck up, tall and fat. A janitor was washing down the front steps. Everything looked new and modern. The houses, the stores, the pavement and sidewalks. The parking meters. A brown-uniformed cop was giving a car a ticket. Trees, growing at intervals. Neatly clipped and pruned.

He passed a big supermarket. Out in front was a bin of fruit, oranges and grapes. He picked a grape and bit into it.

The grape was real, all right. A big black concord grape, sweet and ripe. Yet twenty-four hours ago there had been nothing here but a barren field.

Paine entered one of the drugstores. He leafed through some magazines and then sat down at the counter. He ordered a cup of coffee from the red-cheeked little waitress.

"This is a nice town," Paine said, as she brought the coffee.

"Yes, isn't it?"

Paine hesitated. "How—how long have you been working here?"

"Three months."

"Three months?" Paine studied the buxom little blonde. "You live here in Macon Heights?"

"Oh, yes."

"How long?"

"A couple years, I guess." She moved away to wait on a young soldier who had taken a stool down the counter.

Paine sat drinking his coffee and smoking, idly watching the people passing by outside. Ordinary people. Men and women, mostly women. Some had grocery bags and little wire carts. Automobiles drove slowly back and forth. A sleepy little suburban town. Modern, upper middle-class. A quality town. No slums here. Small, attractive houses. Stores with sloping glass fronts and neon signs.

Some high school kids burst into the drugstore, laughing and bumping into each other. Two girls in bright sweaters sat down next to Paine and ordered lime drinks. They chatted gaily, bits of their conversation drifting to him.

He gazed at them, pondering moodily. They were real, all right. Lipstick and red fingernails. Sweaters and armloads of school books. Hundreds of high school kids, crowding eagerly into the drugstore.

Paine rubbed his forehead wearily. It didn't seem possible. Maybe he was out of his mind. The town was *real.* Completely real. It must have always existed. A whole town couldn't rise up out of nothing; out of a cloud of gray haze. Five thousand people, houses and streets and stores.

Stores. Bradshaw Insurance.

Stabbing realization chilled him. Suddenly he understood. It was spreading. Beyond Macon Heights. Into the city. The city was changing, too. Bradshaw Insurance. Critchet's place of business.

Macon Heights couldn't exist without warping the city. They interlocked. The five thousand people came from the city. Their jobs. Their lives. The city was involved.

But how much? How much was the city changing?

Paine threw a quarter on the counter and hurried out of the drugstore, toward the train station. He had to get back to the city. Laura, the change. Was she still there? Was his *own* life safe?

Fear gripped him. Laura, all his possessions, his plans, hopes and dreams. Suddenly Macon Heights was unimportant. His own world was in jeopardy. Only one thing mattered now. He had to make sure of it; make sure his own life was still there. Untouched by the spreading circle of change that was lapping out from Macon Heights.

"Where to, buddy?" the cabdriver asked, as Paine came rushing out of the train station.

Paine gave him the address of the apartment. The cab roared out into traffic. Paine settled back nervously. Outside the window the streets and office buildings flashed past. White collar workers were already beginning to get off work, swelling out onto the sidewalks to stand in clumps at each corner.

How much had changed? He concentrated on a row of buildings. The big department store. Had that always been there? The little boot-black shop next to it. He had never noticed that before.

NORRIS HOME FURNISHINGS.

He didn't remember *that*. But how could he be sure? He felt confused. How could he tell?

The cab let him off in front of the apartment house. Paine stood for a moment, looking around him. Down at the end of the block the owner of the Italian delicatessen was out putting up the awning. Had he ever noticed a delicatessen there before?

He could not remember.

What had happened to the big meat market across the street? There was nothing but neat little houses; older houses that looked like they'd been there plenty long. Had a meat market ever been there? The houses *looked* solid.

In the next block the striped pole of a barbershop glittered. Had there always been a barbershop there?

Maybe it had always been there. Maybe, and maybe not. Everything was shifting. New things were coming into existence, others going away. The past was altering, and memory was tied to the past. How could he trust his memory? How could he be sure?

Terror gripped him. Laura. His world. . . .

Paine raced up the front steps and pushed open the door of the apartment house. He hurried up the carpeted stairs to the second floor. The door of the apartment was unlocked. He pushed it open and entered, his heart in his mouth, praying silently.

The living room was dark and silent. The shades were half pulled. He glanced around wildly. The light blue couch, magazines on its arms. The low blond-oak table. The television set. But the room was empty.

"Laura!" he gasped.

Laura hurried from the kitchen, eyes wide with alarm. "Bob! What are you doing home? Is anything the matter?"

Paine relaxed, sagging with relief. "Hello, honey." He kissed her, holding her tight against him. She was warm and substantial; completely real. "No, nothing's wrong. Everything's fine."

"Are you sure?"

"I'm sure." Paine took his coat off shakily and dropped it over the back of the couch. He wandered around the room, examining things, his confidence returning. His familiar blue couch, cigarette burns on its arms. His old ragged footstool. His desk where he did his work at night. His fishing rods leaning up against the wall behind the bookcase.

The big television set he had purchased only last month; that was safe, too.

Everything, all he owned, was untouched. Safe. Unharmed.

"Dinner won't be ready for half an hour," Laura murmured anxiously, unfastening her apron. "I didn't expect you home so early. I've just been sitting around all day. I did clean the stove. Some salesman left a sample of a new cleanser."

"That's OK." He examined a favorite Renoir print on the wall. "Take your time. It's good to see all these things again. I—"

From the bedroom a crying sound came. Laura turned quickly. "I guess we woke up Jimmy."

"Jimmy?"

Laura laughed. "Darling, don't you remember your own son?"

"Of course," Paine murmured, annoyed. He followed Laura slowly into the bedroom. "Just for a minute everything seemed strange." He rubbed his forehead, frowning. "Strange and unfamiliar. Sort of out of focus."

They stood by the crib, gazing down at the baby. Jimmy glared back up at his mother and dad.

"It must have been the sun," Laura said. "It's so terribly hot outside."

"That must be it. I'm OK now." Paine reached down and poked at the baby. He put his arm around his wife, hugging her to him. "It must have been the sun," he said. He looked down into her eyes and smiled.

A PRESENT FOR PAT

"WHAT is it?" Patricia Blake demanded eagerly.

"What's what?" Eric Blake murmured.

"What did you bring? I *know* you brought me something!" Her bosom rose and fell excitedly under her mesh blouse. "You brought me a present. I can tell!"

"Honey, I went to Ganymede for Terran Metals, not to find you curios. Now let me unpack my things. Bradshaw says I have to report to the office early tomorrow. He says I better report some good ore deposits."

Pat snatched up a small box, heaped with all the other luggage the robot porter had deposited at the door. "Is it jewelry? No, it's too big for jewelry." She began to tear the cord from the box with her sharp fingernails.

Eric frowned uneasily. "Don't be disappointed, honey. It's sort of strange. Not what you expect." He watched apprehensively. "Don't get mad at me. I'll explain all about it."

Pat's mouth fell open. She turned pale. She dropped the box quickly on the table, eyes wide with horror. "Good Lord! What *is* it?"

Eric twisted nervously. "I got a good buy on it, honey. You can't usually pick one of them up. The Ganymedeans don't like to sell them, and I—"

"What is it?"

"It's a god," Eric muttered. "A minor Ganymedean deity. I got it practically at cost."

Pat gazed down at the box with fear and growing disgust. "That? That's a—a *god?"*

In the box was a small, motionless figure, perhaps ten inches high. It was old, terribly old. Its tiny clawlike hands were pressed against its scaly breast. Its insect face was twisted in a scowl of anger—mixed with cynical lust. Instead of legs it rested on a tangle of tentacles. The lower portion of its face dissolved in a complex beak, mandibles of some hard substance. There was an odor to it, as of manure and stale beer. It appeared to be bisexual.

Eric had thoughtfully put a little water dish and some straw in the box. He had punched air holes in the lid and crumbled up newspaper fragments.

"You mean it's an idol." Pat regained her poise slowly. "An *idol* of a deity."

"No." Eric shook his head stubbornly. "This is a genuine deity. There's a warranty, or something."

"Is it—dead?"

"Not at all."

"Then why doesn't it move?"

"You have to arouse it." The bottom of the figure's belly cupped outward in a hollow bowl. Eric tapped the bowl. "Place an offering here and it comes to life. I'll show you."

Pat retreated. "No thanks."

"Come on! It's interesting to talk to. Its name is—" He glanced at some writing on the box. "It's name is Tinokuknoi Arevulopapo. We talked most of the way back from Ganymede. It was glad of the opportunity. And I learned quite a few things about gods."

Eric searched his pockets and brought out the remains of a ham sandwich. He wadded up a bit of the ham and stuffed it into the protruding belly-cup of the god.

"I'm going in the other room," Pat said.

"Stick around." Eric caught her arm. "It only takes a second. It begins to digest right away."

The belly-cup quivered. The god's scaly flesh rippled. presently the cup filled with a sluggish dark-colored substance. The ham began to dissolve.

Pat snorted in disgust. "Doesn't it even use its mouth?"

"Not for eating. Only for talking. It's a lot different from usual life-forms."

The tiny eye of the god was focused on them now. A single, unwinking orb of icy malevolence. The mandibles twitched.

"Greetings," the god said.

"Hi." Eric nudged Pat forward. "This is my wife. Mrs. Blake. Patricia."

"How do you do," the god grated.

Pat gave a squeal of dismay. "It talks English."

The god turned to Eric in disgust. "You were right. She *is* stupid."

Eric colored. "Gods can do anything they want, honey. They're omnipotent."

The god nodded. "That is so. This is Terra, I presume."

"Yes. How does it look?"

"As I expected. I have already heard reports. Certain reports about Terra."

"Eric, are you sure it's safe?" Pat whispered uneasily. "I don't like its looks. And there's something about the way it talks." Her bosom quivered nervously.

"Don't worry, honey," Eric said carelessly. "It's a nice god. I checked before I left Ganymede."

"I'm benevolent," the god explained matter-of-factly. "My capacity has been that of Weather Deity to the Ganymedean aborigines. I have produced rain and allied phenomena when the occasion demanded."

"But that's all in the past," Eric added.

"Correct. I have been a Weather Deity for ten thousand years. There is a limit to even a god's patience. I craved new surroundings." A peculiar gleam flickered across the loathsome face. "That is why I arranged to be sold and brought to Terra."

"You see," Eric said, "the Ganymedeans didn't want to sell it. But it whipped up a thunderstorm and they sort of had to. That's partly why it was so cheap."

"Your husband made a good purchase," the god said. Its single eye roved around curiously. "This is your dwelling? You eat and sleep here?"

"That's right," Eric said. "Pat and I both—"

The front door chimed. "Thomas Matson stands on the threshold," the door stated. "He wishes admission."

"Golly," Eric said. "Good old Tom. I'll go let him in."

Pat indicated the god. "Hadn't you better—"

"Oh, no. I want Tom to see it." Eric stepped to the door and opened it.

"Hello," Tom said, striding in. "Hi, Pat. Nice day." He and Eric shook hands. "The Lab has been wondering when you'd get back. Old Bradshaw is leaping up and down to hear your report." Matson's bean-pole body bent forward in sudden interest. "Say, what's in the box?"

"That's my god," Eric said modestly.

"Really? But God is an unscientific concept."

"This is a different god. I didn't invent it. I bought it. On Ganymede. It's a Ganymedean Weather Deity."

"Say something," Pat said to the god. "So he'll believe your owner."

"Let's debate my existence," the god said sneeringly. "You take the negative. Agreed?"

Matson grinned. "What is this, Eric? A little robot? Sort of hideous looking."

"Honest. It's a god. On the way it did a couple of miracles for me. Not big miracles, of course, but enough to convince me."

"Hearsay," Matson said. But he was interested. "Pass a miracle, god. I'm all ears."

"I am not a vulgar showpiece," the god growled.

"Don't get it angry," Eric cautioned. "There's no limit to its powers, once aroused."

"How does a god come into being?" Tom asked. "Does a god create itself? If it's dependent on something prior then there must be a more ultimate order of being which—"

"Gods," the tiny figure stated, "are inhabitants of a higher level, a greater plane of reality. A more advanced dimension. There are a number of planes of existence. Dimensional continuums, arranged in a hierarchy. Mine is one above yours."

"What are you doing here?"

"Occasionally beings pass from one dimensional continuum to another. When they pass from a superior continuum to an inferior—as I have done—they are worshiped as gods."

Tom was disappointed. "You're not a god at all. You're just a life-form of a slightly different dimensional order that's changed phase and entered our vector."

The little figure glowered. "You make it sound simple. Actually, such a transformation requires great cunning and is seldom done. I came here because a member of my race, a certain malodorous Nar Dolk, committed a heinous crime and escaped into this continuum. Our law obliged me to follow in hot pursuit. In the process this flotsam, this spawn of dampness, escaped and assumed some disguise or other. I continually search, but he has not yet been apprehended." The small god broke off suddenly. "Your curiosity is idle. It annoys me."

Tom turned his back on the god. "Pretty weak stuff. We do more down at the Terran Metals Lab than this character ever—"

The air cracked, ozone flashing. Tom Matson shrieked. Invisible hands lifted him bodily and propelled him to the door. The door swung open and Matson sailed down the walk, tumbling in a heap among the rose bushes, arms and legs flailing wildly.

"Help!" Matson yelled, struggling to get up.

"Oh, dear," Pat gasped.

"Golly." Eric shot a glance at the tiny figure. "You did that?"

"Help him," Pat urged, white-faced. "I think he's hurt. He looks funny."

Eric hurried outside and helped Matson to his feet. "You OK? It's your own fault. I told you if you kept annoying it something might happen."

Matson's face was ablaze with rage. "No little pipsqueak god is going to treat me like this!" He pushed Eric aside, heading back for the house. "I'll take it down to the Lab and pop it in a bottle of formaldehyde. I'll dissect it and skin it and hang it up on the wall. I'll have the first specimen of a god known to—"

A ball of light glowed around Matson. The ball enveloped him, settling in place around his lean body so that he looked like a filament in an incandescent light.

"What the hell!" Matson muttered. Suddenly he jerked. His body faded. He began to shrink. With a faint whoosh he diminished rapidly. Smaller and smaller he dwindled. His body shuddered, altering strangely.

The light winked out. Sitting stupidly on the walk was a small green toad.

"See?" Eric said wildly. "I told you to keep quiet! Now look what it's done!"

The toad hopped feebly toward the house. At the porch

it sagged into immobility, defeated by the steps. It uttered a pathetic, hopeless *chug*.

Pat's voice rose in a wail of anguish. "Oh, Eric! Look what it's done! Poor Tom!"

"His own fault," Eric said. "He deserves it." But he was beginning to get nervous. "Look here," he said to the god. "That's not a very nice thing to do to a grown man. What'll his wife and kids think?"

"What'll Mr. Bradshaw think?" Pat cried. "He can't go to work like that!"

"True," Eric admitted. He appealed to the god. "I think he's learned his lesson. How about turning him back? OK?"

"You just better undo him!" Pat shrieked, clenching her small fists. "If you don't undo him you'll have Terran Metals after you. Even a god can't stand up to Horace Bradshaw."

"Better change him back," Eric said.

"It'll do him good," the god said. "I'll leave him that way for a couple of centuries—"

"Centuries!" Pat exploded. "Why, you little blob of slime!" She advanced ominously toward the box, shaking with wrath. "See here! You turn him back or I'll take you out of your box and drop you into the garbage disposal unit!"

"Make her be still," the god said to Eric.

"Calm down, Pat," Eric implored.

"I will not calm down! Who does it think it is? A present! How *dare* you bring this moldy bit of refuse into our house? Is this your idea of a—"

Her voice ceased abruptly.

Eric turned apprehensively. Pat stood rigid, her mouth open, a word still on her lips. She did not move. She was white all over. A solid gray-white that made cold chills leap up Eric's spine. "Good Lord," he said.

"I turned her to stone," the god explained. "She made too much noise." It yawned. "Now, I think I'll retire. I'm a little tired, after my trip."

"I can't believe it," Eric Blake said. He shook his head numbly. "My best friend a toad. My wife turned to stone."

"It's true," the god said. "We deal out justice according to how people act. They both got what they deserved."

"Can—can she hear me?"

"I suppose."

Eric went over to the statue. "Pat," he begged imploringly. "Please don't be mad. It isn't my fault." He gripped her ice-cold shoulders. "Don't blame me! I didn't do it." The granite was hard and smooth under his fingers. Pat stared blankly ahead.

"Terran Metals indeed," the god grumbled sourly. Its single eye studied Eric intently. "Who is this Horace Bradshaw? Some local deity, perhaps?"

"Horace Bradshaw owns Terran Metals," Eric said gloomily. He sat down and shakily lit a cigarette. "He's about the biggest man on Terra. Terran Metals owns half the planets in the system."

"Kingdoms of this world do not interest me," the god said noncommittally, subsiding and shutting its eye. "I will retire now. I wish to contemplate certain matters. You may wake me later, if you wish. We can converse on theological subjects, as we did on the ship coming here."

"Theological subjects," Eric said bitterly. "My wife a stone block and it wants to talk about religion."

But the god was already withdrawn, retired into itself.

"A lot you care," Eric muttered. Anger flickered in him. "This is the thanks I get for taking you off Ganymede. Ruin my household and my social life. Fine god you are!"

No response.

Eric concentrated desperately. Maybe when the god awoke it would be in a better mood. Maybe he could persuade it to turn Matson and Pat back to their usual forms. Faint hope stirred. He could appeal to the god's better side. After it had rested and slept for a few hours. . . .

If nobody came looking for Matson.

The toad sat disconsolately on the walk, drooping with misery. Eric leaned toward it. "Hey, Matson!"

The toad looked slowly up.

"Don't worry, old man. I'll get it to turn you back. It's a cinch." The toad didn't stir. "A lead-pipe cinch," Eric repeated nervously.

The toad drooped a little more. Eric looked at his watch. It was late afternoon, almost four. Tom's shift at Terran began in half an hour. Sweat came out on his forehead. If the god went on sleeping and didn't wake up in half an hour—

A buzz. The vidphone.

Eric's heart sank. He hurried over and clicked the screen on, steeling himself. Horace Bradshaw's sharp, dignified features faded into focus. His keen glance bored into Eric, penetrating his depths.

"Blake," he grunted. "Back from Ganymede, I see."

"Yes, sir." Eric's mind raced frantically. He moved in front of the screen, cutting off Bradshaw's view of the room. "I'm just starting to unpack."

"Forget that and get over here! We're waiting to hear your report."

"Right now? Gosh, Mr. Bradshaw. Give me a chance to get my things away." He fought desperately for time. "I'll be over tomorrow morning bright and early."

"Is Matson there with you?"

Eric swallowed. "Yes, sir. But—"

"Put him on. I want to talk to him."

"He—he can't talk to you right now, sir."

"What? Why not?"

"He's in no shape to—that is, he—"

Bradshaw snarled impatiently. "Then bring him along with you. And he better be sober when he gets here. I'll see you at my office in ten minutes." He broke the circuit. The screen faded abruptly.

Eric sank wearily down in a chair. His mind reeled. Ten minutes! He shook his head, stunned.

The toad hopped a little, stirring on the walk. It emitted a faint, despondent sound.

Eric got heavily to his feet. "I guess we have to face the music," he murmured. He bent down and picked up the toad, putting it gingerly in his coat pocket. "I guess you heard. That was Bradshaw. We're going down to the lab."

The toad stirred uneasily.

"I wonder what Bradshaw is going to say when he sees you." Eric kissed his wife's cold granite cheek. "Good-bye, honey." He moved numbly down the walk to the street. A moment later he hailed a robot cab and entered it. "I have a feeling this is going to be hard to explain." The cab zipped off down the street. "Hard as hell to explain."

Horace Bradshaw stared in dumbfounded amazement. He removed his steel-rimmed glasses and wiped them slowly. He fitted them back on his hard, hawklike face and peered down. The toad rested silently in the center of the immense mahogany desk.

Bradshaw pointed shakily at the toad. "This—this is Thomas Matson?"

"Yes, sir," Eric said.

Bradshaw blinked in wonder. "Matson! What in the world has happened to you?"

"He's a toad," Eric explained.

"So I see. Incredible." Bradshaw pressed a stud on his desk. "Send in Jennings from the Biology Lab," he ordered. "A toad." He poked the toad with his pencil. "Is it really you, Matson?"

The toad *chugged.*

"Good Lord." Bradshaw sat back, wiping his forehead. His grim expression faded into sympathetic concern. He shook his head sadly. "I can't believe it. Some kind of bacterial blight, I suppose. Matson was always experimenting on himself. He took his work seriously. A brave man. A good worker. He did much for Terran Metals. Too bad he had to end this way. We'll extend full pension to him, of course."

Jennings entered the office. "You wanted me, sir?"

"Come in." Bradshaw beckoned him impatiently in. "We have a problem for your department. You know Eric Blake here."

"Hi, Blake."

"And Thomas Matson." Bradshaw indicated the toad. "From the Nonferrous Lab."

"I know Matson," Jennings said slowly. "That is, I know a Matson from Nonferrous. But I don't recall—that is, he was taller than this. Almost six feet."

"This is him," Eric said gloomily. "He's a toad now."

"What happened?" Jennings' scientific curiosity was aroused. "What's the lowdown?"

"Its a long story," Eric said evasively.

"Can't you tell it?" Jennings scrutinized the toad professionally. "Looks like a regular type of toad. You're sure this is Tom Matson? Come clean, Blake. You must know more than you're telling!"

Bradshaw studied Eric intently. "Yes, what *did* happen, Blake? You have a strange, shifty look. Are you responsible for this?" Bradshaw half rose from his chair, his grim face bleak. "See here. If it's your fault one of my best men has been incapacitated for further work—"

"Take it easy," Eric protested, his mind racing frantically. He patted the toad nervously. "Matson is perfectly safe—as long as nobody steps on him. We can rig up some sort of protective shield and an automatic communication system that'll enable him to spell out words. He can continue his work. With a few adjustments here and there everything should speed along perfectly."

"Answer me!" Bradshaw roared. "Are you responsible for this? Is this *your* doing?"

Eric squirmed helplessly. "In a way, I suppose. Not exactly. Not *directly*." His voice wavered. "But I guess you'd say if it hadn't been for me . . ."

Bradshaw's face set in a rigid mask of rage. "Blake, you're fired." He yanked a heap of forms from his desk dispenser. "Get out of here and never come back. And get your hand off that toad. It belongs to Terran Metals." He shoved a paper across the desk. "Here's your paycheck. And don't bother looking for work elsewhere. I'm listing you on the inter-system blacklist. Good day."

"But, Mr. Bradshaw—"

"Don't plead." Bradshaw waved his hand. "Just go. Jennings, get your biology staff busy at once. This problem must be licked. I want you to rearrange this toad back to its original shape. Matson is a vital part of Terran Metals. There's work to be done, work only Matson can do. We can't have this sort of thing holding up our research."

"Mr. Bradshaw," Eric begged desperately. "Please listen. I want to see Tom back as he was. But there's only one way we can get him back his original shape. We—"

Bradshaw's eyes were cold with hostility. "You still here, Blake? Must I call my guards and have you dismembered? I'm giving you one minute to be off Company land. Understand?"

Eric nodded miserably. "I understand." He turned and

shuffled unhappily toward the door. "So long, Jennings. So long, Tom. I'll be home if you want me, Mr. Bradshaw."

"Sorcerer," Bradshaw snapped. "Good riddance."

"What would you do," Eric asked the robot cabdriver, "if your wife had turned to stone, your best friend were a toad, and you had lost your job?"

"Robots have no wives," the driver said. "They are nonsexual. Robots have no friends, either. They are incapable of emotional relationships."

"Can robots be fired?"

"Sometimes." The robot drew his cab up before Eric's modest six-room bungalow. "But consider. Robots are frequently melted down and new robots made from the remains. Recall Ibsen's *Peer Gynt,* the section concerning the Button Molder. The lines clearly anticipate in symbolic form the trauma of robots to come."

"Yeah." The door opened and Eric got out. "I guess we all have our problems."

"Robots have worse problems than anybody." The door shut and the cab zipped off, back down the hill.

Worse? Hardly. Eric entered his home slowly, the front door automatically opening for him.

"Welcome, Mr. Blake," the door greeted him.

"I suppose Pat's still here."

"Mrs. Blake is here, but she is in a cataleptic state, or some similar condition."

"She's been turned to stone." Eric kissed the cold lips of the statue gloomily. "Hi, honey."

He got some meat from the refrigerator and crumbled it into the belly-cup of the god. Presently digestive fluid rose and covered the food. In a short time the single eye of the god opened, blinked a few times, and focused on Eric.

"Have a good sleep?" Eric inquired icily.

"I wasn't asleep. My mind was turned toward matters of cosmic import. I detect a hostile quality in your voice. Has something unfavorable occurred?"

"Nothing. Nothing at all. I just lost my job, on top of everything else."

"Lost your job? Interesting. What else do you refer to?"

Eric exploded in rage. "You've messed up my whole life, damn you!" He jabbed at the silent, unmoving figure of his wife. "Look! My wife! Turned to granite. And my best friend, a toad."

Tinokuknoi Arevulopapo yawned. "So?"

"*Why?* What did I ever do to you? Why do you treat me this way? Look at all I've done for you. I only brought you here to Terra. Fed you. Fixed you up a box with straw and water and newspapers. That's all."

"True. You did bring me to Terra." Again an odd gleam flickered across the god's dark face. "All right. I'll restore your wife."

"You will?" Pathetic joy surged through Eric. Tears came to his eyes. He was too relieved to ask any questions. "Gosh, I sure would appreciate it!"

The god concentrated. "Stand out of the way. It's easier to distort the molecular arrangement of a body than to restore the original configuration. I hope I can get it exactly as it was." It made a faint motion.

Around Pat's silent figure the air stirred. The pale granite shuddered. Slowly, color seeped back into her features. She gasped sharply, her dark eyes flashing with fear. Color filled her arms, shoulders, breasts, spreading through her trim body. She cried out, tottering unsteadily. "*Eric!*"

Eric caught her, hugging her tight. "Gosh, honey. I'm sure glad you're all right." He crushed her against him, feeling her heart thump with terror. He kissed her soft lips again and again. "Welcome back."

Pat pulled abruptly away. "That little snake. That miserable particle of waste. Wait until I get my hands on it." She advanced toward the god, eyes blazing. "Listen, you. What's the idea? How *dare* you!"

"See?" the god said. "They never change."

Eric pulled his wife back. "You better shut up or you'll be granite again. Understand?"

Pat caught the urgent rasp in his voice. She subsided reluctantly. "All right, Eric. I give up."

"Listen," Eric said to the god. "How about Tom? How about restoring him?"

"The toad? Where is he?"

"In the Biology Lab. Jennings and his staff are working on him."

The god considered. "I don't like the sound of that. The Biology Lab? Where is that? How far away?"

"Terran Metals. Main Building." Eric was impatient. "Maybe five miles. How about it? Maybe if you restore him Bradshaw will give me my job back. You owe it to me. Set things back the way they were."

"I can't."

"You *can't!* Why the hell not?"

"I thought gods were omnipotent," Pat sniffed petulantly.

"I can do anything—at short range. The Terran Metals Biology Lab is too far. Five miles is beyond my limit. I can distort molecular arrangements within a limited circle only."

Eric was incredulous. "What? You mean you can't turn Tom back?"

"That's the way it is. You shouldn't have taken him out of the house. Gods are subject to natural law just as you are. Our laws are different, but they are still laws."

"I see," Eric murmured. "You should have said."

"As far as your job goes, don't worry about that. Here, I'll create some gold." The god made a motion with its scaly hands. A section of curtain flashed suddenly yellow and crashed to the floor with a metallic tinkle. "Solid gold. That ought to keep you a few days."

"We're no longer on the gold standard."

"Well, whatever you need. I can do anything."

"Except turn Tom back into a human being," Pat said. "Fine god you are."

"Shut up, Pat," Eric muttered, deep in thought.

"If there were some way I could be closer to him," the god said cautiously. "If he were within range. . ."

"Bradshaw will never let him go. And I can't set foot around there. The guards will tear me to bits."

"How about some platinum?" The god made a pass and a section of the wall glowed white. "Solid platinum. A simple change of atomic weight. Will that help?"

"No!" Eric paced back and forth. "We've got to get that toad away from Bradshaw. If we can get him back here—"

"I have an idea," the god said.

"What?"

"Perhaps you could get me in there. Perhaps if I could get onto the Company grounds, within range of the Biology Lab. . ."

"It's worth a try," Pat said, putting her hand on Eric's shoulder. "After all, Tom's your best friend. It's a shame to treat him this way. It's—it's un-Terran."

Eric grabbed his coat. "It's settled. I'll drive as close as I can to the Company grounds. I ought to be able to get near enough before the guards catch sight of me to—"

A crash. The front door collapsed abruptly in a heap of ash. Teams of robot police surged into the room, blastguns ready.

"All right," Jennings said. "That's him." He strode quickly into the house. "Get him. And get that thing in the box."

"Jennings!" Eric swallowed in alarm. "What the hell is this?"

Jennings' lip curled. "Cut out the pretense, Blake. You're not fooling me." He tapped a small metal case under his arm. "The toad revealed all. So you've got a non-Terrestrial in this house, have you?" He laughed coldly. "There's a law against bringing non-Terrans to Earth. You're under arrest, Blake. You'll probably get life."

"Tinokuknoi Arevulopapo!" Eric Blake squeaked. "Don't forsake me at a time like this!"

"I'm coming," the god grunted. It heaved violently. "How's this?"

The robot police jerked as a torrent of force erupted from the box. Abruptly they disappeared, winking out of existence. Where they had stood a horde of mechanical mice milled aimlessly, spilling frantically through the doorway, out into the yard.

Jennings' face showed astonishment and then panic. He retreated, waving his blaster menacingly. "See here, Blake. Don't think you can scare me. We've got this house surrounded."

A bolt of force hit him in the stomach. The bolt lifted him and shook him like a rag doll. His blaster skidded from his fingers, falling to the floor. Jennings groped for it desperately. The blaster turned into a spider and crawled rapidly off, out of his reach.

"Set him down," Eric urged.

"All right." The god released Jennings. He crashed to the floor, stunned and frightened. He scrambled wildly to his feet and ran from the house, down the path to the sidewalk.

"Oh dear," Pat said.

"What is it?"

"Look."

Pulled up in a circle around the house was a solid line of atomic cannon. Their snouts gleamed wickedly in the late afternoon sunlight. Groups of robot police stood around each cannon, waiting alertly for instructions.

Eric groaned. "We're sunk. One blast and we're finished."

"Do something!" Pat gasped. She prodded the box. "Enchant them. Don't just sit there."

"They are out of range," the god replied. "As I explained, my power is limited by distance."

"You in there!" a voice came, magnified by a hundred loudspeakers. "Come out with your hands up. Or we open fire!"

"Bradshaw," Eric groaned. "He's out there. We're trapped. You sure you can't do something?"

"Sorry," the god said. "I can put up a shield against the cannon." It concentrated. Outside the house a dull surface formed, a globe rapidly hardening around them.

"All right," Bradshaw's magnified voice came, muffled by the shield. "You asked for it."

The first shell hit. Eric found himself lying on the floor, his ears ringing, everything going around and around. Pat lay beside him, dazed and frightened. The house was a shambles. Walls, chairs, furniture, all was in ruins.

"Fine shield," Pat gasped.

"The concussion," the god protested. Its box lay in the corner on its side. "The shield stops the shells, but the concussion—"

A second shell struck. A wall of pressure rolled over Eric, stunning him. He skidded, tossed by a violent wind, crashing against heaps of debris that had been his house.

"We can't last," Pat said faintly. "Tell them to stop, Eric. Please!"

"Your wife is right," the god's calm voice came, from its overturned box. "Surrender, Eric. Give yourself up."

"I guess I better." Eric pulled himself up on his knees. "But golly, I don't want to spend the rest of my life in prison. I knew I was breaking the law when I smuggled the damn thing in here, but I never thought—"

A third shell hit. Eric tumbled down, his chin smacking the floor. Plaster and rubble rained down on him, choking and blinding him. He fought his way up, grabbing hold of a jutting beam.

"Stop!" he shouted.

There was sudden silence.

"Are you willing to surrender?" the magnified voice boomed.

"Surrender," the god murmured.

Eric's mind raced desperately. "I—I have a deal. A compromise." He thought fast, his brain in high gear. "I have a proposal."

There was a long pause. "What's the proposal?"

Eric stepped warily through the rubble to the edge of the shield. The shield was almost gone. Only a shimmering haze remained, through which the circle of atomic cannon was visible, the cannon and the robot police.

"Matson," Eric gasped, getting his breath. "The toad. We'll make the following deal. We'll restore Matson to his original shape. We'll return the non-Terrestrial to Ganymede. In return, you waive prosecution and I get my job back."

"Absurd! My labs can easily restore Matson without your help."

"Oh yeah? Ask Matson. He'll tell you. If you don't agree, Matson will be a toad for the next two hundred years—at least!"

A long silence followed. Eric could see figure moving back and forth, conferring behind the guns.

"All right," Bradshaw's voice came at last. "We agree. Drop the shield and come forward. I'll send Jennings with the toad. No tricks, Blake!"

"No tricks." Eric sagged with relief. "Come along," he said to the god, picking up the dented box. "Drop the shield and let's get this over with. Those cannon make me nervous."

The god relaxed. The shield—what was left of it—wavered and faded, blinking off.

"Here I come." Eric advanced warily, the box in his hands. "Where's Matson?"

Jennings came toward him. "I have him." His curiosity overcame his suspicion. "This ought to be interesting. We should make a close study of all extra-dimensional life. Apparently they possess science much in advance of our own."

Jennings squatted down, placing the small green toad carefully on the grass.

"There he is," Eric said to his god.

"Is this close enough?" Pat asked icily.

"This is sufficient," the god said. "This is exactly right." It turned its single eye on the toad and made a few brief motions with its scaly claws.

A shimmer hovered over the toad. Extra-dimensional forces were at work, fingering and plucking at the toad molecules. Abruptly the toad twitched. For a second it shuddered, an insistent vibration lapped over it. Then—

Matson ballooned into existence, the familiar bean-pole figure, towering over Eric and Jennings and Pat.

"Lord," Matson breathed shakily. He got out his handkerchief and wiped his face. "I'm glad that's over. Wouldn't want to go through that again."

Jennings retreated hurriedly toward the circle of cannon. Matson turned and headed after him. Eric and his wife and god were suddenly alone in the center of the lawn.

"Hey!" Eric demanded, cold alarm plucking at him. "What is this? What the hell's going on?"

"Sorry, Blake," Bradshaw's voice came. "It was essential to restore Matson. But we can't alter the law. The law is above any man, even me. You're under arrest."

Robot police swarmed forward, grimly surrounding Eric and Pat. "You skunk," Eric choked, struggling feebly.

Bradshaw came out from behind the cannon, hands in his pockets, grinning calmly. "Sorry, Blake. You should be out of jail in ten or fifteen years, though. Your job will be waiting for you—I promise. As for this extra-dimensional being, I'm quite interested in seeing it. I've heard of such things." He peered toward the box. "I'm happy to take charge of it. Our labs will perform experiments and tests on it which will. . ."

Bradshaw's words died. His face turned a sickly hue. His mouth opened and closed, but no sounds came.

From the box came a swelling, frenzied buzz of rage. *"Nar Dolk!* I knew I'd find you!"

Bradshaw retreated, trembling violently. "Why, of all persons. Tinokuknoi Arevulopapo! What are you doing on Terra?" He stumbled, half falling. "How did you, that is, after so long, how could—"

Then Bradshaw was running, scattering robot police in all directions, rushing wildly past the atomic cannon.

"Nar Dolk!" the god screamed, swelling with fury. "Scourge of the Seven Temples! Flotsam of Space! I knew you were on this miserable planet! Come back and take your punishment!"

The god burst upward, flashing into the air. It raced past Eric and Pat, growing as it flew. A sickening, nauseous wind, warm and damp, lapped at their faces, as the god gained speed.

Bradshaw—Nar Dolk—ran frantically. And as he ran he *changed.* Immense wings sprouted from him. Great leathery wings, beating the air in frantic haste. His body oozed and altered. Tentacles replaced legs. Scaly claws replaced arms. Gray hide rippled as he flew up, wings flapping noisily.

Tinokuknoi Arevulopapo struck. For a brief moment the two locked together, twisting and rolling in the air, wings and claws raking and flapping.

Then Nar Dolk broke away, fluttering up. A blazing flash, a pop, and he was gone.

For a moment Tinokuknoi Arevulopapo hovered in the air. The scaly head turned, the single eye glancing back and down at Eric and Pat. It nodded briefly. Then, with a curious shimmy, it vanished.

The sky was empty except for a few feathers and the dull stench of burning scales.

Eric was the first to speak. "Well," he said. "So that's why it wanted to come to Terra. I guess I was sort of exploited." He grinned sheepishly. "The first Terran ever to be exploited."

Matson gawked, still peering up. "They're gone. Both of them. Back to their own dimension, I guess."

A robot policeman plucked at Jennings' sleeves. "Shall we arrest anyone, sir? With Mr. Bradshaw gone you are next in charge."

Jennings glanced at Eric and Pat. "I suppose not. The evidence has departed. It seems somewhat silly, anyhow." He shook his head. "Bradshaw. Imagine! And we worked for him for years. Damn strange business."

Eric put his arm around his wife. He pulled her against him, hugging her tight. "I'm sorry, honey," he said softly.

"Sorry?"

"Your present. It's gone. I guess I'll have to get you something else."

Pat laughed, pressing against him. "That's all right. I'll let you in on a secret."

"What?"

Pat kissed him, her lips warm against his cheek. "As a matter of fact—I'm just as glad."

BREAKFAST AT TWILIGHT

"DAD?" Earl asked, hurrying out of the bathroom, "you going to drive us to school today?"

Tim McLean poured himself a second cup of coffee. "You kids can walk for a change. The car's in the garage."

Judy pouted. "It's raining."

"No it isn't," Virginia corrected her sister. She drew the shade back. "It's all foggy, but it isn't raining."

"Let me look." Mary McLean dried her hands and came over from the sink. "What an odd day. Is that fog? It looks more like smoke. I can't make out a thing. What did the weather man say?"

"I couldn't get anything on the radio," Earl said. "Nothing but static."

Tim stirred angrily. "That darn thing on the blink again? Seems like I just had it fixed." He got up and moved sleepily over to the radio. He fiddled idly with the dials. The three children hurried back and forth, getting ready for school. "Strange," Tim said.

"I'm going." Earl opened the front door.

"Wait for your sisters," Mary ordered absently.

"I'm ready," Virginia said. "Do I look all right?"

"You look fine," Mary said, kissing her.

"I'll call the radio repair place from the office," Tim said.

He broke off. Earl stood at the kitchen door, pale and silent, his eyes wide with terror.

"What is it?"

"I—I came back."

"What is it? Are you sick?"

"I can't go to school."

They stared at him. "What is wrong?" Tim grabbed his son's arm. "Why can't you go to school?"

"They—they won't let me."

"Who?"

"The soldiers."

It came tumbling out with a rush. "They're all over. Soldiers and guns. And they're coming here."

"Coming? Coming here?" Tim echoed, dazed.

"They're coming here and they're going to—" Earl broke off, terrified. From the front porch came the sound of heavy boots. A crash. Splintering wood. Voices.

"Good Lord," Mary gasped. "What is it, Tim?"

Tim entered the living room, his heart laboring painfully. Three men stood inside the door. Men in gray-green uniforms, weighted with guns and complex tangles of equipment. Tubes and hoses. Meters on thick cords. Boxes and leather straps and antennas. Elaborate masks locked over their heads. Behind the masks Tim saw tired, whisker-stubbled faces, red-rimmed eyes that gazed at him in brutal displeasure.

One of the soldiers jerked up his gun, aiming at McLean's middle. Tim peered at it dumbly. *The gun.* Long and thin. Like a needle. Attached to a coil of tubes.

"What in the name of—" he began, but the soldier cut him off savagely.

"Who are you?" His voice was harsh, guttural. "What are you doing here?" He pushed his mask aside. His skin was dirty. Cuts and pocks lined his sallow flesh. His teeth were broken and missing.

"Answer!" a second soldier demanded. "What are you doing here?"

"Show your blue card," the third said. "Let's see your Sector number." His eyes strayed to the children and Mary standing mutely at the dining room door. His mouth fell open.

"A woman!"

The three soldiers gazed in disbelief.

"What the hell is this?" the first demanded. "How long has this woman been here?"

Tim found his voice. "She's my wife. What is this? What—"

"Your *wife?"* They were incredulous.

"My wife and children. For God's sake—"

"Your wife? And you'd bring her here? You must be out of your head!"

"He's got ash sickness," one said. He lowered his gun and strode across the living room to Mary. "Come on, sister. You're coming with us."

Tim lunged.

A wall of force hit him. He sprawled, clouds of darkness rolling around him. His ears sang. His head throbbed. Everything receded. Dimly, he was aware of shapes moving. Voices. The room. He concentrated.

The soldiers were herding the children back. One of them grabbed Mary by the arm. He tore her dress away, ripping it from her shoulders. "Gee," he snarled. "He'd bring her here, and she's not even stung!"

"Take her along."

"OK, Captain." The soldier dragged Mary toward the front door. "We'll do what we can with her."

"The kids." The captain waved the other soldier over with the children. "Take them along. I don't get it. No masks. No cards. How'd this house miss getting hit? Last night was the worst in months!"

Tim struggled painfully to his feet. His mouth was bleeding. His vision blurred. He hung on tight to the wall. "Look," he muttered. "For God's sake—"

The captain was staring into the kitchen. "Is that—is that *food?*" He advanced slowly through the dining room. "Look!"

The other soldiers came after him, Mary and the children forgotten. They stood around the table, amazed.

"Look at it!"

"Coffee." One grabbed up the pot and drank it greedily down. He choked, black coffee dripping down his tunic. "Hot. Jeeze. Hot coffee."

"Cream!" Another soldier tore open the refrigerator. "Look. Milk. Eggs. Butter. Meat." His voice broke. "It's full of food."

The captain disappeared into the pantry. He came out, lugging a case of canned peas. "Get the rest. Get it all. We'll load it in the snake."

He dropped the case on the table with a crash. Watching Tim intently, he fumbled in his dirty tunic until he found a cigarette. He lit it slowly, not taking his eyes from Tim. "All right," he said. "Let's hear what you have to say."

Tim's mouth opened and closed. No words came. His mind was blank. Dead. He couldn't think.

"This food. Where'd you get it? And these things." The captain waved around the kitchen. "Dishes. Furniture. How come this house hasn't been hit? How did you survive last night's attack?"

"I—" Tim gasped.

The captain came toward him ominously. "The woman. And the kids. All of you. What are you doing here?" His voice was hard. "You better be able to explain, mister. You better be able to explain what you're doing here—or we'll have to burn the whole damn lot of you."

Tim sat down at the table. He took a deep, shuddering breath, trying to focus his mind. His body ached. He rubbed blood from his mouth, conscious of a broken molar and bits of loose tooth. He got out a handkerchief and spat the bits into it. His hands were shaking.

"Come on," the captain said.

Mary and the children slipped into the room. Judy was crying. Virginia's face was blank with shock. Earl stared wide-eyed at the soldiers, his face white.

"Tim," Mary said, putting her hand on his arm. "Are you all right?"

Tim nodded. "I'm all right."

Mary pulled her dress around her. "Tim, they can't get away with it. Somebody'll come. The mailman. The neighbors. They can't just—"

"Shut up," the captain snapped. His eyes flickered oddly. "The mailman? What are you talking about?" He held out his hand. "Let's see your yellow slip, sister."

"Yellow slip?" Mary faltered.

The captain rubbed his jaw. "No yellow slip. No masks. No cards."

"They're geeps," a soldier said.

"Maybe. And maybe not."

"They're geeps, Captain. We better burn 'em. We can't take any chances."

"There's something funny going on here," the captain

said. He plucked at his neck, lifting up a small box on a cord. "I'm getting a polic here."

"A polic?" A shiver moved through the soldiers. "Wait, Captain. We can handle this. Don't get a polic. He'll put us on 4 and then we'll never—"

The captain spoke into the box. "Give me Web B."

Tim looked up at Mary. "Listen, honey. I—"

"Shut up." A soldier prodded him. Tim lapsed into silence.

The box squawked. "Web B."

"Can you spare a polic? We've run into something strange. Group of five. Man, woman, three kids. No masks, no cards, the woman not stung, dwelling completely intact. Furniture, fixtures, and about two hundred pounds of food."

The box hesitated. "All right. Polic on his way. Stay there. Don't let them escape."

"I won't." The captain dropped the box back in his shirt. "A polic will be here any minute. Meanwhile, let's get the food loaded."

From outside came a deep thundering roar. It shook the house, rattling the dishes in the cupboard.

"Jeez," a soldier said. "That was close."

"I hope the screens hold until nightfall." The captain grabbed up the case of canned peas. "Get the rest. We want it loaded before the polic comes."

The two soldiers filled their arms and followed him through the house, out the front door. Their voices diminished as they strode down the path.

Tim got to his feet. "Stay here," he said thickly.

"What are you doing?" Mary asked nervously.

"Maybe I can get out." He ran to the back door and unlatched it, hands shaking. He pulled the door wide and stepped out on the back porch. "I don't see any of them. If we can only . . ."

He stopped.

Around him gray clouds blew. Gray ash, billowing as far as he could see. Dim shapes were visible. Broken shapes, silent and unmoving in the grayness.

Ruins.

Ruined buildings. Heaps of rubble. Debris everywhere. He walked slowly down the back steps. The concrete walk ended abruptly. Beyond it, slag and heaps of rubble were strewn. Nothing else. Nothing as far as the eye could see.

Nothing stirred. Nothing moved. In the gray silence there was no life. No motion. Only the clouds of drifting ash. The slag and the endless heaps.

The city was gone. The buildings were destroyed. Nothing remained. No people. No life. Jagged walls, empty and gaping. A few dark weeds growing among the debris. Tim bent down, touching a weed. Rough, thick stalk. And the slag. It was metal slag. Melted metal. He straightened up—

"Come back inside," a crisp voice said.

He turned numbly. A man stood on the porch, behind him, hands on his hips. A small man, hollow-cheeked. Eyes small and bright, like two black coals. He wore a uniform different from the soldiers'. His mask was pushed back, away from his face. His skin was yellow, faintly luminous, clinging to his cheekbones. A sick face, ravaged by fever and fatigue.

"Who are you?" Tim said.

"Douglas. Political Commissioner Douglas."

"You're—you're the polic," Tim said.

"That's right. Now come inside. I expect to hear some answers from you. I have quite a few questions.

"The first thing I want to know," Commissioner Douglas said, "is how this house escaped destruction."

Tim and Mary and the children sat together on the couch, silent and unmoving, faces blank with shock.

"Well?" Douglas demanded.

Tim found his voice. "Look," he said. "I don't know. I don't know anything. We woke up this morning like every other morning. We dressed and ate breakfast—"

"It was foggy out," Virginia said. "We looked out and saw the fog."

"And the radio wouldn't work," Earl said.

"The radio?" Douglas' thin face twisted. "There haven't been any audio signals in months. Except for government purposes. This house. All of you. I don't understand. If you were geeps—"

"Geeps. What does that mean?" Mary murmured.

"Soviet general-purpose troops."

"Then the war has begun."

"North America was attacked two years ago," Douglas said. "In 1978."

Tim sagged. "1978. Then this is 1980." He reached suddenly into his pocket. He pulled out his wallet and tossed it to Douglas. "Look in there."

Douglas opened the wallet suspiciously. "Why?"

"The library card. The parcel receipts. Look at the dates." Tim turned to Mary. "I'm beginning to understand now. I had an idea when I saw the ruins."

"Are we winning?" Earl piped.

Douglas studied Tim's wallet intently. "Very interesting. These are all old. Seven and eight years." His eyes flickered. "What are you trying to say? That you came from the past? That you're time travelers?"

The captain came back inside. "The snake is all loaded, sir."

Douglas nodded curtly. "All right. You can take off with your patrol."

The captain glanced at Tim. "Will you be—"

"I'll handle them."

The Captain saluted. "Fine, sir." He quickly disappeared through the door. Outside, he and his men climbed aboard a long thin truck, like a pipe mounted on treads. With a faint hum the truck leaped forward.

In a moment only gray clouds and the dim outline of ruined buildings remained.

Douglas paced back and forth, examining the living room, the wall paper, the light fixtures and chairs. He picked up some magazines and thumbed through them. "From the past. But not far in the past."

"Seven years."

"Could it be? I suppose. A lot of things have happened in the last few months. Time travel." Douglas grinned ironically. "You picked a bad spot, McLean. You should have gone farther on."

"I didn't pick it. It just happened."

"You must have done *something.*"

Tim shook his head. "No. Nothing. We got up. And we were—here."

Douglas was deep in thought. "Here. Seven years in the future. Moved forward through time. We know nothing about time travel. No work has been done with it. There seem to be no evident military possibilities."

"How did the war begin?" Mary asked faintly.

"Begin? It didn't begin. You remember. There was war seven years ago."

"The real war. This."

"There wasn't any point when it became—this. We fought in Korea. We fought in China. In Germany and Yugoslavia and Iran. It spread, farther and farther. Finally the bombs were falling here. It came like the plague. The war *grew*. It didn't begin." Abruptly he put his notebook away. "A report on you would be suspect. They might think I had the ash sickness."

"What's that?" Virginia asked.

"Radioactive particles in the air. Carried to the brain. Causes insanity. Everybody has a touch of it, even with the masks."

"I'd sure like to know who's winning," Earl repeated. "What was that outside? That truck. Was it rocket propelled?"

"The snake? No. Turbines. Boring snout. Cuts through the debris."

"Seven years," Mary said. "So much has changed. It doesn't seem possible."

"So much?" Douglas shrugged. "I suppose so. I remember what I was doing seven years ago. I was still in school. Learning. I had an apartment and a car. I went out dancing. I bought a TV set. But these things were there. The twilight. This. Only I didn't know. None of us knew. But they were there."

"You're a Political Commissioner?" Tim asked.

"I supervise the troops. Watch for political deviation. In a total war we have to keep people under constant surveillance. One Commie down in the Webs could wreck the whole business. We can't take chances."

Tim nodded. "Yes. It was there. The twilight. Only we didn't understand it."

Douglas examined the books in the bookcase. "I'll take a couple of these along. I haven't seen fiction in months. Most of it disappeared. Burned back in '77."

"Burned?"

Douglas helped himself. "Shakespeare. Milton. Dryden.

I'll take the old stuff. It's safer. None of the Steinbeck and Dos Passos. Even a polic can get in trouble. If you stay here, you better get rid of *that*." He tapped a volume of Dostoevski, *The Brothers Karamazov*.

"If we stay! What else can we do?"

"You want to stay?"

"No," Mary said quietly.

Douglas shot her a quick glance. "No, I suppose not. If you stay you'll be separated, of course. Children to the Canadian Relocation Centers. Women are situated down in the undersurface factory-labor camps. Men are automatically a part of Military."

"Like those three who left," Tim said.

"Unless you can qualify for the id block."

"What's that?"

"Industrial designing and Technology. What training have you had? Anything along scientific lines."

"No. Accounting."

Douglas shrugged. "Well, you'll be given a standard test. If your IQ is high enough you could go in the Political Service. We use a lot of men." He paused thoughtfully, his arms loaded with books. "You better go back, McLean. You'll have trouble getting accustomed to this. I'd go back, if I could. But I can't."

"Back?" Mary echoed. "How?"

"The way you came."

"We just came."

Douglas halted at the front door. "Last night was the worst rom attack so far. They hit this whole area."

"Rom?"

"Robot operated missiles. The Soviets are systemically destroying continental America, mile by mile. Roms are cheap. They make them by the million and fire them off. The whole process is automatic. Robot factories turn them out and fire them at us. Last night they came over here—waves of them. This morning the patrol came in and found nothing. Except you, of course."

Tim nodded slowly. "I'm beginning to see."

"The concentrated energy must have tipped some unstable time-fault. Like a rock fault. We're always starting earthquakes. But a *time quake* . . . interesting. That's what happened, I think. The release of energy, the destruction of matter, sucked your house into the future. Carried the house seven years ahead. This street, everything here, this very spot, was pulverized. Your house, seven years back, was caught in the undertow. The blast must have lashed back through time."

"Sucked into the future," Tim said. "During the night. While we were asleep."

Douglas watched him carefully. "Tonight," he said, "there will be another rom attack. It should finish off what is left." He looked at his watch. "It is now four in the afternoon. The attack will begin in a few hours. You should be undersurface. Nothing will survive up here. I can take you down with me, if you want. But if you want to take a chance, if you want to stay here—"

"You think it might tip us back?"

"Maybe. I don't know. It's a gamble. It might tip you back to your own time, or it might not. If not—"

"If not we wouldn't have a chance of survival."

Douglas flicked out a pocket map and spread it open on the couch. "A patrol will remain in this area another half hour. If you decide to come undersurface with us, go down this street this way." He traced a line on the map. "To this open field here. The patrol is a Political unit. They'll take you the rest of the way down. You think you can find the field?"

"I think so," Tim said, looking at the map. His lips twisted. "That open field used to be the grammar school my kids went to. That's where they were going when the troops stopped them. Just a little while ago."

"Seven years ago," Douglas corrected. He snapped the map shut and restored it to his pocket. He pulled his mask down and moved out the front door onto the porch. "Maybe I'll see you again. Maybe not. It's your decision. You'll have to decide one way or the other. In any case—good luck."

He turned and walked briskly away from the house.

"Dad," Earl shouted, "are you going in the Army? Are you going to wear a mask and shoot one of those guns?" His eyes sparkled with excitement. "Are you going to drice a *snake?*"

Tim McLean squatted down and pulled his son to him. "You want that? *You want to stay here?* If I'm going to wear a mask and shoot one of those guns we can't go back."

Earl looked doubtful. "Couldn't we go back later?"

Tim shook his head. "Afraid not. We've got to decide now, whether we're going back or not."

"You heard Mr. Douglas," Virginia said disgustedly. "The attack's going to start in a couple of hours."

Tim got to his feet and paced back and forth. "If we stay in the house we'll get blown to bits. Let's face it. There's only a faint chance we'll be tipped back to our own time. A slim possibility—a long shot. Do we want to stay here with roms falling all around us, knowing any second it may be the end—hearing them come closer, hitting nearer—lying on the floor, waiting, listening—"

"Do you really want to go back?" Mary demanded.

"Of course, but the risk—"

"I'm not asking you about the risk. I'm asking you if you really want to go back. Maybe you want to stay here. Maybe Earl's right. You in a uniform and a mask, with one of those needle guns. Driving a snake."

"With you in a factory-labor camp! And the kids in a Government Relocation Center! How do you think that would be? What do you think they'd teach them? What do you think they'd grow up like? And believe. . . ."

"They'd probably teach them to be very useful."

"Useful! To what? To themselves? To mankind? Or to the war effort. . . ?"

"They'd be alive," Mary said. "They'd be safe. This way, if we stay in the house, wait for the attack to come—"

"Sure," Tim grated. "They would be alive. Probably quite healthy. Well fed. Well clothed and cared for." He looked down at his children, his face hard. "They'd stay alive, all right. They'd live to grow up and become adults. But what kind of adults? You heard what he said! Book burnings in '77. What'll they be taught from? What kind of ideas are left, since '77? What kind of beliefs can they get from a Government Relocation Center? What kind of values will they have?"

"There's the id block," Mary suggested.

"Industrial designing and Technology. For the bright ones. The clever ones with imagination. Busy slide rules and pencils. Drawing and planning and making discoveries. The girls could go into that. They could design the guns. Earl could go into the Political Service. He could make sure the guns were used. If any of the troops deviated, didn't want to shoot, Earl could report them and have them hauled off for reeducation. To have their political faith strengthened—in a world where those *with* brains design weapons and those *without* brains fire them."

"But they'd be alive," Mary repeated.

"You've got a strange idea of what being alive is! You call that alive? Maybe it is." Tim shook his head wearily. "Maybe you're right. Maybe we should go undersurface with Douglas. Stay in this world. Stay alive."

"I didn't say that," Mary said softly. "Tim, I had to find out if you *really* understood why it's worth it. Worth staying in the house, taking the chance we won't be tipped back."

"Then you want to take the chance?"

"Of course! We *have* to. We can't turn our children over to them—to the Relocation Center. To be taught how to hate and kill and destroy." Mary smiled up wanly. "Anyhow, they've always gone to the Jefferson School. And here, in this world. it's only an open field."

"Are we going back?" Judy piped. She caught hold of Tim's sleeve imploringly. "Are we going back now?"

Tim disengaged her arm. "Very soon, honey."

Mary opened the supply cupboards and rooted in them. "Everything's here. What did they take?"

"The case of canned peas. Everything we had in the refrigerator. And they smashed the front door."

"I'll bet we're beating them!" Earl shouted. He ran to the window and peered out. The sight of the rolling ash disappointed him. "I can't see anything! Just the fog!" He turned questioningly to Tim. "Is it always like this, here?"

"Yes," Tim answered.

Earl's face fell. "Just fog? Nothing else? Doesn't the sun shine ever?"

"I'll fix some coffee," Mary said.

"Good." Tim went into the bathroom and examined himself in the mirror. His mouth was cut, caked with dried blood. His head ached. He felt sick at his stomach.

"It doesn't seem possible," Mary said, as they sat down at the kitchen table.

Tim sipped his coffee. "No. It doesn't." Where he sat he could see out the window. The clouds of ash. The dim, jagged outline of ruined buildings.

"Is the man coming back?" Judy piped. "He was all thin and funny-looking. He isn't coming back, is he?"

Tim looked at his watch. It read ten o'clock. He reset it, moving the hands to four-fifteen. "Douglas said it would begin at nightfall. That won't be long."

"Then we're really staying in the house," Mary said.

"That's right."

"Even though there's only a little chance?"

"Even though they's only a little chance we'll get back. Are you glad?"

"I'm glad," Mary said, her eyes bright. "It's worth it, Tim. You know it is. Anything's worth it, any chance. *To get back*. And something else. We'll all be here together. . . . We can't be—broken up. Separated."

Tim poured himself more coffee. "We might as well make ourselves comfortable. We have maybe three hours to wait. We might as well try to enjoy them."

At six-thirty the first rom fell. They felt the shock, a deep rolling wave of force that lapped over the house.

Judy came running from the dining room, face white with fear. "Daddy! What is it?"

"Nothing. Don't worry."

"Come on back," Virginia called impatiently. "It's your turn." They were playing Monopoly.

Earl leaped to his feet. "I want to see." He ran excitedly to the window. "I can see where it hit!"

Tim lifted the shade and looked out. Far off, in the distance, a white glare burned fitfully. A towering column of luminous smoke rose from it.

A second shudder vibrated through the house. A dish crashed from the shelf, into the sink.

It was almost dark outside. Except for the two spots of white Tim could make out nothing. The clouds of ash were lost in the gloom. The ash and the ragged remains of buildings.

"That was closer," Mary said.

A third rom fell. In the living room the windows burst, showering glass across the rug.

"We better get back," Tim said.

"Where?"

"Down in the basement. Come on." Tim unlocked the basement door and they trooped nervously downstairs.

"Food," Mary said. "We better bring the food that's left."

"Good idea. You kids go on down. We'll come along in a minute."

"I can carry something," Earl said.

"Go on down." The fourth rom hit, farther off than the last. "And stay away from the window."

"I'll move something over the window," Earl said. "The big piece of plywood we used for my train."

"Good idea." Tim and Mary returned to the kitchen. "Food. Dishes. What else?"

"Books." Mary looked nervously around. "I don't know. Nothing else. Come on."

A shattering roar drowned out her words. The kitchen window gave, showering glass over them. The dishes over the sink tumbled down in a torrent of breaking china. Tim grabbed Mary and pulled her down.

From the broken window rolling clouds of ominous gray drifted into the room. The evening air stank, a sour, rotten smell. Tim shuddered.

"Forget the food. Let's get back down."

"But—"

"Forget it." He grabbed her and pulled her down the basement stairs. They tumbled in a heap, Tim slamming the door after them.

"Where's the food?" Virginia demanded.

Tim wiped his forehead shakily. "Forget it. We won't need it."

"Help me," Earl gasped. Tim helped him move the sheet of plywood over the window above the laundry tubs. The basement was cold and silent. The cement floor under them was faintly moist.

Two roms struck at once. Tim was hurled to the floor. The concrete hit him and he grunted. For a moment blackness swirled around him. Then he was on his knees, groping his way up.

"Everybody all right?" he muttered.

"I'm all right," Mary said. Judy began to whimper. Earl was feeling his way across the room.

"I'm all right," Virginia said. "I guess."

The lights flickered and dimmed. Abruptly they went out. The basement was pitch-black.

"Well," Tim said. "There they go."

"I have my flashlight." Earl winked the flashlight on. "How's that?"

"Fine," Tim said.

More roms hit. The ground leaped under them, bucking and heaving. A wave of force shuddering the whole house.

"We better lie down," Mary said.

"Yes. Lie down." Tim stretched himself out awkwardly. A few bits of plaster rained down around them.

"When will it stop?" Earl asked uneasily.

"Soon," Tim said.

"Then we'll be back?"

"Yes. We'll be back."

The next blast hit them almost at once. Tim felt the concrete rise under him. It grew, swelling higher and higher. He was going up. He shut his eyes, holding on tight. Higher and higher he went, carried up by the ballooning concrete. Around him beams and timbers cracked. Plaster poured down. He could hear glass breaking. And a long way off, the licking crackles of fire.

"Tim," Mary's voice came faintly.

"Yes."

"We're not going to—to make it."

"I don't know."

"We're not. I can tell."

"Maybe not." He grunted in pain as a board struck his back, settling over him. Boards and plaster, covering him, burying him. He could smell the sour smell, the night air and ash. It drifted and rolled into the cellar, through the broken window.

"Daddy," Judy's voice came faintly.

"What?"

"Aren't we going back?"

He opened his mouth to answer. A shattering roar cut his words off. He jerked, tossed by the blast. Everything was moving around him. A vast wind tugged at him, a hot wind, licking at him, gnawing at him. He held on tight. The wind pulled, dragging him with it. He cried out as it seared his hands and face.

"Mary—"

Then silence. Only blackness and silence.

Cars.

Cars were stopping nearby. Then voices. And the noise of footsteps. Tim stirred, pushing the boards from him. He struggled to his feet.

"Mary." He looked around. "We're back."

The basement was in ruins. The walls were broken and sagging. Great gaping holes showed a green line of grass beyond. A concrete walk. The small rose garden. The white side of the stucco house next door.

Lines of telephone poles. Roofs. Houses. The city. As it had always been. Every morning.

"We're back!" Wild joy leaped through him. *Back*. Safe. It was over. Tim pushed quickly through the debris of his ruined house. "Mary, are you all right?"

"Here." Mary sat up, plaster dust raining from her. She was white all over, her hair, her skin, her clothing. Her face was cut and scratched. Her dress was torn. "Are we really back?"

"Mr. McLean! You all right?"

A blue-clad policeman leaped down into the cellar. Behind him two white-clad figures jumped. A group of neighbors collected outside, peering anxiously to see.

"I'm OK," Tim said. He helped Judy and Virginia up. "I think we're all OK."

"What happened?" The policeman pushed boards aside, coming over. "A bomb? Some kind of a bomb?"

"The house is a shambles," one of the white-clad interns said. "You sure nobody's hurt?"

"We were down here. In the basement."

"You all right, Tim?" Mrs. Hendricks called, stepping down gingerly into the cellar.

"What happened?" Frank Foley shouted. He leaped down with a crash. "God, Tim! What the hell were you doing?"

The two white-clad interns poked suspiciously around the ruins. "You're lucky, mister. Damn lucky. There's nothing left upstairs."

Foley came over beside Tim. "Damn it man! I *told* you to have that hot water heater looked at!"

"What?" Tim muttered.

"The hot water heater! I told you there was something wrong with the cut-off. It must've kept heating up, not turned off. . . ." Foley winked nervously. "But I won't say anything, Tim. The insurance. You can count on me."

Tim opened his mouth. But the words didn't come. What could he say? —No, it wasn't a defective hot water heater that I forgot to have repaired. No, it wasn't a faulty connection in the stove. It wasn't any of those things. It wasn't a leaky gas line, it wasn't a plugged furnace, it wasn't a pressure cooker we forgot to turn off.

It's war. Total war. And not just war for me. For my family. For just my house.

It's for your house, too. Your house and my house and all the houses. Here and in the next block, in the next town, the next state and country and continent. The whole world, like this. Shambles and ruins. Fog and dank weeds growing in the rusting slag. War for all of us. For everybody crowding down into the basement, white-faced, frightened, somehow sensing something terrible.

And when it really came, when the five years were up, there'd be no escape. No going back, tipping back into the past, away from it. When it came for them all, it would have them for eternity; there would be no one climbing back out, as he had.

Mary was watching him. The policeman, the neighbors, the white-clad interns—all of them were watching him. Waiting for him to explain. To tell them what it was.

"Was it the hot water heater?" Mrs. Hendricks asked timidly. "That was it, wasn't it, Tim? Things like that do happen. You can't be sure. . . ."

"Maybe it was home brew," a neighbor suggested, in a feeble attempt at humor. "Was that it?"

He couldn't tell them. They wouldn't understand, because they didn't want to understand. They didn't want to know. They needed reassurance. He could see it in their eyes. Pitiful, pathetic fear. They sensed something terrible—and they were afraid. They were searching his face, seeking his help. Words of comfort. Words to banish their fear.

"Yeah," Tim said heavily. "It was the hot water heater."

"I thought so!" Foley breathed. A sigh of relief swept through them all. Murmurs, shaky laughs. Nods, grins.

"I should have got it fixed," Tim went on. "I should have had it looked at a long time ago. Before it got in such bad shape." Tim looked around at the circle of anxious people, hanging on his words. "I should have had it looked at. Before it was too late."

SHELL GAME

A SOUND awoke O'Keefe instantly. He threw back his covers, slid from the cot, grabbed his B-pistol from the wall and, with his foot, smashed the alarm box. High frequency waves tripped emergency bells throughout the camp. As O'Keefe burst from his house, lights already flickered on every side.

"Where?" Fisher demanded shrilly. He appeared beside O'Keefe, still in his pajamas, grubby-faced with sleep.

"Over to the right." O'Keefe leaped aside for a massive cannon being rolled from its underground storage-chambers. Soldiers were appearing among the night-clad figures. To the right lay the black bog of mists and obese foliage, ferns and pulpy onions, sunk in the half-liquid ooze that made up the surface of Betelgeuse II. Nocturnal phosphorescence danced and flitted over the bog, ghostly yellow lights snapped in the thick darkness.

"I figure," Horstokowski said, "they came in close to the road, but not actually on it. There's a shoulder fifty feet on each side, where the bog has piled up. That's why our radar's silent."

An immense mechanical fusing "bug" was eating its way into the mud and shifting water of the bog, leaving behind a trail of hard, smoked surface. The vegetation and the rotting roots and dead leaves were sucked up and efficiently cleared away.

"What did you see?" Portbane asked O'Keefe.

"I didn't see anything. I was sound asleep. But I *heard* them."

"Doing what?'

"They were getting ready to pump nerve gas into my house. I heard them unreeling the hose from portable drums and uncapping the pressure tanks. But, by God, I was out of the house before they could get the joints leak-tight!"

Daniels hurried up. "You say it's a gas attack?" He fumbled for the gas mask at his belt. "Don't stand there—get your masks on!"

"They didn't get their equipment going," Silberman said. "O'Keefe gave the alarm in time. They retreated back to the bog."

"You're sure?" Daniels demanded.

"You don't smell anything, do you?"

"No," Daniels admitted. "But the odorless type is the most deadly. And you don't know you've been gassed till it's too late." He put on his gas mask, just to be sure.

A few women appeared by the rows of houses—slim, large-eyed shapes in the flickering glare of the emergency searchlights. Some children crept cautiously after them.

Silberman and Horstokowski moved over in the shadows by the heavy cannon.

"Interesting," Horstokowski said. "Third gas attack this month. Plus two tries to wire bomb terminals within the camp site. They're stepping it up."

"You have it all figured out, don't you?"

"I don't have to wait for the composite to see we're getting it heavier all the time." Horstokowski peered warily around, then pulled Silberman close. "Maybe there's a reason why the radar screen didn't react. It's supposed to get everything, even knocker-bats."

"But if they came in along the shoulder, like you said—"

"I just said that as a plant. *There's somebody waving them in, setting up interference for the radar.*"

"You mean one of us?"

Horstokowski was intently watching Fisher through the moist night gloom. Fisher had moved carefully to the edge of the road, where the hard surface ended and the slimy, scorched bog began. He was squatting down and rooting in the ooze.

"What's he doing?" Horstokowski demanded.

"Picking up something," Silberman said indifferently. "Why not? He's supposed to be looking around, isn't he?"

"Watch," Horstokowski warned. "When he comes back, he's going to pretend nothing happened."

Presently, Fisher returned, walking rapidly and rubbing the muck from his hands.

Horstokowski intercepted him. "What'd you find?"

"Me?" Fisher blinked. "I didn't find anything."

"Don't kid me! You were down on your hands and knees, grubbing in the bog."

"I—thought I saw something metal, that's all."

A vast inner excitement radiated through Horstokowski. He had been right.

"Come on!" he shouted. "What'd you find?"

"I thought it was a gas pipe," Fisher muttered. "But it was only a root. A big, wet root."

There was a tense silence.

"Search him," Portbane ordered.

Two soldiers grabbed Fisher. Silberman and Daniels quickly searched him.

They spilled out his belt pistol, knife, emergency whistle, automatic relay checker, Geiger counter, pulse tab, medical kit and identification papers. There was nothing else.

The soldiers let him go, disappointed, and Fisher sullenly collected his things.

"No, he didn't find anything," Portbane stated. "Sorry, Fisher. We have to be careful. We have to watch all the time, as long as they're out there, plotting and conspiring against us."

Silberman and Horstokowski exchanged glances, then moved quietly away.

"I think I get it," Silberman said softly.

"Sure," Horstokowski answered. "He *hid* something. We'll dig up that section of bog he was poking around in. I think maybe we'll find something interesting." He hunched his shoulders combatively. "I knew somebody was working for them, here in the camp. A spy for Terra."

Silberman started. "Terra? Is that who's attacking us?"

"Of course that's who."

There was a puzzled look on Silberman's face.

"Seemed to me we're fighting somebody else."

Horstokowski was outraged.

"For instance?"

Silberman shook his head. "I don't know. I didn't think about who so much as what to do about it. I guess I just took it for granted they were aliens."

"And what do you think those Terran monkey men are?" Horstokowski challenged.

The weekly Pattern Conference brought together the nine leaders of the camp in their reinforced underground conference chamber. Armed guards protected the entrance, which was sealed tight as soon as the last leader had been examined, checked over and finally passed.

Domgraf-Schwach, the conference chairman, sat attentively in his deep chair, one hand on the Pattern composite, the other on the switch that could instantly catapult him from the room and into a special compartment, safe from attack. Portbane was making his routine inspection of the chamber, examining each chair and desk for scanning eyes. Daniels sat with eyes fixed on his Geiger counter. Silberman was completely encased in an elaborate steel and plastic suit, configured with wiring, from which continual whirrings came.

"What in God's name is that suit of armor?" Domgraf-Schwach asked angrily. "Take it off so we can see you."

"Nuts to you," Silberman snapped, his voice muted by his intricate hull. "I'm wearing this from now on. Last night, somebody tried to jab me with bacteria-impregnated needles."

Lanoir, who was half-dozing at his place, came alive. "Bacteria-impregnated needles?" He leaped up and hurried over to Silberman. "Let me ask you if—"

"Keep away from me!" Silberman shouted. "If you come any closer, I'll electrocute you!"

"The attempt I reported last week," Lanoir panted excitedly, "when they tried to poison the water supply with metallic salts. It occurred to me their next method would be bacterial wastes, filterable virus we couldn't detect until actual outbreak of disease." From his pocket, he yanked a bottle and shook out a handful of white capsules. One after another, he popped the capsules into his mouth.

Every man in the room was protected in some fashion. Each chose whatever apparatus conformed to his individual experience. But the totality of defense-systems was integrated in the general Pattern planning. The only man who didn't seem busy with a device was Tate. He sat pale and tense, but otherwise unoccupied. Domgraf-Schwach made a mental note—Tate's confidence-level was unusually high. It suggested he somehow felt safe from attack.

"No talking," Domgraf-Schwach said. "Time to start."

He had been chosen as chairman by the turn of a wheel. There was no possibility of subversion under such a system. In an isolated, autonomous colony of sixty men and fifty women, such a random method was necessary.

"Daniels will read the week's Pattern composite," Domgraf-Schwach ordered.

"Why?" Portbane demanded bluntly. "We were the ones who put it together. We all know what's in it."

"For the same reason it's always read," Silberman answered. "So we'll know it wasn't tampered with."

"Just the summation!" Horstokowski said loudly. "I don't want to stay down here in this vault any longer than I have to."

"Afraid somebody'll fill up the passage?" Daniels jeered. "There are half a dozen emergency escape exits. You ought to know—you insisted on every one of them."

"Read the summation," Lanoir demanded.

Daniels cleared his throat. "During the last seven days, there were eleven overt attacks in all. The main attack was on our new class-A bridge network, which was sabotaged and wrecked. The struts were weakened and the plastic mix that served as base material was diluted, so that when the very first convoy of trucks passed over it, the whole thing collapsed."

"We know that," Portbane said gloomily.

"Loss consisted of six lives and considerable equipment. Troops scoured the area for a whole day, but the saboteurs managed to escape. Shortly after this attack, it was discovered that the water supply was poisoned with metallic salts. The wells were therefore filled and new ones drilled. Now all our water passes through filter and analysis systems."

"I boil mine," Lanoir added feelingly.

"It's agreed by everyone that the frequency and severity of attacks have been stepped up." Daniels indicated the massive wall charts and graphs. "Without our bomb-proof screen and our constant direction network, we'd be overwhelmed tonight. The real quesiton is—*who are our attackers?*"

"Terrans," Horstokowski said.

Tate shook his head. "Terrans, hell! What would monkey men be doing out this far?"

"We're out this far, aren't we?" Lanoir retorted. "And we were Terrans once."

"Never!" Fisher shouted. "Maybe we lived on Terra, but we aren't Terrans. We're a superior mutant race."

"Then who are they?" Horstokowski insisted.

"They're other survivors from the ship," Tate said.

"How do you know?" asked Silberman. "Have you ever seen them?"

"We salvaged no lifeboats, remember? They must have blasted off in them."

"If they were isolated survivors," O'Keefe objected, "they wouldn't have the equipment and weapons and machines they're using. They're a trained, integrated force. We haven't been able to defeat them or even *kill* any of them in five years. That certainly shows their strength."

"We haven't tried to defeat them," Fisher said. "We've only tried to defend ourselves."

A sudden tense silence fell over the nine men.

"You mean the ship," Horstokowski said.

"It'll be up out of the bog soon," Tate replied. "And then we'll have something to show them—something they'll remember."

"Good God!" Lanoir exclaimed, disgusted. "The ship's a wreck—the meteor completely smashed it. What happens when we do get it up? We can't operate it unless we can completely rebuild it."

"If the monkey men could build the thing," Portbane said, "we can repair it. We have the tools and machinery."

"And we've finally located the control cabin," O'Keefe pointed out. "I see no reason why we can't raise it."

There was an abrupt change of expression on Lanoir's face. "All right, I withdraw my objections. Let's get it up."

"What's your motive?" Daniels yelled excitedly. "You're trying to put something over on us!"

"He's planning something," Fisher furiously agreed. "Don't listen to him. Leave the damn thing down there!"

"Too late for that," O'Keefe said. "It's been rising for weeks."

"You're in with him!" Daniels screeched. "Something's being put over on us."

The ship was a dripping, corroded ruin. Slime poured from it as the magnetic grapples dragged it from the bog and onto the hard surface that the fusing bugs had laid down.

The bugs burned a hard track through the bog, out to the control cabin. While the lift suspended the cabin, heavy reinforced plastic beams were slid under it. Tangled weeds, matted like ancient hair, covered the globular cabin in the midday sun, the first light that had struck it in five years.

"In you go," Domgraf-Schwach said eagerly.

Portbane and Lanoir advanced over the fused surface to the moored control cabin. Their handlights flashed ominously yellow around the steaming walls and encrusted controls. Livid eels twisted and convulsed in the thick pools underfoot. The cabin was a smashed, twisted ruin. Lanoir, who was first, motioned Portbane impatiently after him.

"*You* look at these controls—you're the engineer."

Portbane set down his light on a sloping heap of rusted metal and sloshed through the knee-deep rubbish to the demolished control panel. It was a maze of fused, buckled machinery. He squatted down in front of it and began tearing away the pitted guard-plates.

Lanoir pushed open a supply closet and brought down metal-packed audio and video tapes. He eagerly spilled open a can of the video and held a handful of frames to the flickering light. "Here's the ship's data. Now I'll be able to prove there was nobody but us aboard."

O'Keefe appeared at the jagged doorway. "How's it coming?"

Lanoir elbowed past him and out on the support boards. He deposited a load of tape-cans and returned to the drenched cabin. "Find anything on the controls?" he asked Portbane.

"Strange," Portbane murmured.

"What's the matter?" Tate demanded. "Too badly wrecked?"

"There are lots of wires and relays. Plenty of meters and power circuits and switches. But no controls to operate them."

Lanoir hurried over. "There must be!"

"For repairs, you have to remove all these plates—practically dismantle the works to even see them. Nobody could sit here and control the ship. There's nothing but a smooth, sealed shell."

"Maybe this wasn't the control cabin," Fisher offered.

"This is the steering mechanism—no doubt about that." Portbane pulled out a heap of charred wiring. "But all this was self-contained. They're robot controls. Automatic."

They looked at each other.

"Then we were prisoners," Tate said, dazed.

"Whose?" Fisher asked baffledly.

"The Terrans!" Lanoir said.

"I don't get it," Fisher muttered vaguely. "*We* planned the whole flight—didn't we? We broke out of Ganymede and got away."

"Get the tapes going," Portbane said to Lanoir. "Let's see what's in them."

Daniels snapped the vidtape scanner off and raised the light.

"Well," he said, "you saw for yourselves this was a hospital ship. It carried no crew. It was directed from a central guide-beam at Jupiter. The beam carried it from the Sol System here, where, because of a mechanical error, a meteor penetrated the protection screen and the ship crashed."

"And if it hadn't crashed?" Domgraf-Schwach asked faintly.

"Then we would have been taken to the main hospital at Fomalhaut IV."

"Play the last tape again," Tate urged.

The wall-speaker spluttered and then said smoothly: "The distinction between paranoids and paranoiac syndromes in other psychotic personality disorders must be borne in mind when dealing with these patients. The paranoid retains his general personality structure unimpaired.

Outside of the region of his complex, he is logical, rational, even brilliant. He can be talked to—he can discuss himself—he is aware of his surroundings.

"The paranoid differs from other psychotics in that he remains actively oriented to the outside world. He differs from so-called normal personality types in that he has a set of fixed ideas, false postulates from which he has relentlessly constructed an elaborate system of beliefs, logical and consistent with these false postulates."

Shakily, Daniels interrupted the tape. "These tapes were for the hospital authorities on Fomalhaut IV. Locked in a supply closet in the control cabin. The control cabin itself was sealed off from the rest of the ship. None of us was able to enter it."

"The paranoid is totally rigid," the calm voice of the Terran doctor continued. "His fixed ideas cannot be shaken. They dominate his life. He logically weaves all events, all persons, all chance remarks and happenings, into his system. He is convinced the world is plotting against him—that he is a person of unusual importance and ability against whom endless machinations are directed. To thwart these plots, the paranoid goes to infinite lengths to protect himself. He repeatedly vidtapes the authorities, constantly moves from place to place and, in the dangerous final phases, may even become—"

Silberman snapped it off savagely and the chamber was silent. The nine leaders of the camp sat unmoving in their places.

"We're a bunch of nuts," Tate said finally. "A shipload of psychos who got wrecked by a chance meteor."

"Don't kid yourself," Horstokowski snapped. "There wasn't anything chance about that meteor."

Fisher giggled hysterically. "More paranoid talk. Good God, all these attacks—hallucinations—all in our minds!"

Lanoir poked vaguely at the piles of tape. "What are we to believe? *Are there any attackers?*"

"We've been defending ourselves against them for five years!" Portbane retorted. "Isn't that proof enough?"

"Have you ever seen them?" Fisher asked slyly.

"We're up against the best agents in the Galaxy. Terran shock troops and military spies, carefully trained in subversion and sabotage. They're too clever to show themselves."

"They wrecked the bridge-system," O'Keefe said. "It's true we didn't see them, but the bridge is sure as hell in ruins."

"Maybe it was badly built," Fisher pointed out. "Maybe it just collapsed."

"Things don't 'just collapse'! There's a reason for all these things that have been happening."

"Like what?" Tate demanded.

"Weekly poison gas attacks," Portbane said. "Metallic wastes in the water supply, to name only two."

"And bacteriological crystals," Daniels added.

"Maybe none of these things exist," Lanoir argued. "But how are we to prove it? If we're all insane, *how would we know?*"

"There are over a hundred of us," Domgraf-Schwach said. "We've all experienced these attacks. Isn't that proof enough?"

"A myth can be picked up by a whole society, believed and taught to the next generation. Gods, fairies, witches—believing a thing doesn't make it true. For centuries, Terrans believed the Earth was flat."

"If all foot-rulers grow to thirteen inches," Fisher asked, "how would anybody know? One of them would have to stay twelve inches long, a nonvariable, a constant. We're a bunch of inaccurate rulers, each thirteen inches long. We need one nonparanoid for comparison."

"Or maybe this is all part of their strategy," Silberman said. "Maybe they rigged up that control cabin and planted those tapes there."

"This ought to be no different from trying to test any belief," Portbane explained. "What's the characteristic of a scientific test?"

"It can be duplicated," Fisher said promptly. "Look, we're going around in circles. *We're trying to measure ourselves.* You can't take your ruler, either twelve inches or thirteen inches long, and ask it to measure itself. No instrument can test its own accuracy."

"Wrong," Portbane answered calmly. "I can put together a valid, objective test."

"There's no such test!" Tate shouted excitedly.

"There sure as hell is. And inside of a week, I'll have it set up."

"Gas!" the soldier shouted. On all sides, sirens wailed into life. Women and children scrambled for their masks. Heavy-duty cannon rumbled up from subsurface chambers and took up positions. Along the perimeter of the bog, the fusing bugs were searing away a ribbon of muck. Searchlights played out into the fern-thick darkness.

Portbane snapped off the cock of the steel tank and signaled the workmen. The tank was rolled quickly away from the sea of mud and seared weeds.

"All right," Portbane gasped. "Get it below."

He emerged in the subsurface chamber as the cylinder was being rolled into position.

"That cylinder," Portbane said, "should contain hydrocyanic vapor. It's a sampling made at the site of the attack."

"This is useless," Fisher complained. "They're attacking and here we stand!"

Portbane signaled the workmen and they began laying out the test apparatus. "There will be two samples, precipitates of different vapors, each clearly marked and labeled A and B. One comes from the cylinder filled at the scene of the attack. The other is condensed from air taken out of this room."

"Suppose we describe both as negative?" Silberman asked worriedly. "Won't that throw your test off?"

"Then we'll take more tests. After a couple of months, if we still haven't got anything but negative findings, then the attack hypothesis is destroyed."

"We may see both as positive," Tate said, perplexed.

"In that case, we're dead right now. If we see both samples as positive, I think the case for the paranoid hypothesis has been proved."

After a moment, Domgraf-Schwach reluctantly agreed. "One is the control. If we maintain that it isn't possible to get a control sample that is free of hydrocyanic acid . . ."

"Pretty damn slick," O'Keefe admitted. "You start from the one known factor—our own existence. We can't very well doubt *that*."

"Here are all the choices," Portbane said. "Both positive

means we're psychotic. Both negative means either the attack was a false alarm or there are no attackers. One positive and one negative would indicate there are real attackers, that we're fully sane and rational." He glanced around at the camp leads. *"But we'll all have to agree which sample is which."*

"Our reactions will be recorded secretly?" Tate asked.

"Tabulated and punched by the mechanical eye. Tallied by machinery. Each of us will make an individual discrimination."

After a pause, Fisher said, "I'll try it." He came forward, leaned over the colorimeter and studied the two samples intently. He alternated them for a time and then firmly grabbed the check-stylus.

"You're sure?" Domgraf-Schwach asked. "You really know which is the negative control sample?"

"I know." Fisher noted his findings on the punch sheet and moved away.

"I'm next," Tate said, impatiently pushing up. "Let's get this over with."

One by one, the men examined the two samples, recorded their findings, and then moved off to stand waiting uneasily.

"All right," Portbane said finally. "I'm the last one." He peered down briefly, scribbled his results, then pushed the equipment away. "Give me the readings," he told the workmen by the scanner.

A moment later, the findings were flashed up for everyone to see.

Fisher	A
Tate	A
O'Keefe	B
Horstokowski	B
Silberman	B
Daniels	B
Portbane	A
Domgraf-Schwach	B
Lanoir	A

"I'll be damned," Silberman said softly. "As simple as that. We're paranoids."

"You cluck!" Tate shouted at Horstokowski. "It was A, not B! How the hell could you get it wrong?"

"B was as bright as a searchlight!" Domgraf-Schwach answered furiously. "A was completely colorless!"

O'Keefe pushed forward. "Which was it, Portbane? Which was the positive sample?"

"I don't know," Portbane confessed. "How could any of us be sure?"

The buzzer on Domgraf-Schwach's desk clicked and he snapped on the vidscreen.

The face of a soldier-operator appeared. "The attack's over, sir. We drove them away."

Domgraf-Schwach smiled ironically. "Catch any of them?"

"No, sir. They slipped back into the bog. I think we hit a couple, though. We'll go out tomorrow and try to find the corpses."

"You think you'll find them?"

"Well, the bog usually swallows them up. But maybe this time—"

"All right," Domgraf-Schwach interrupted. "If this turns out to be an exception, let me know." He broke the circuit.

"Now what?" Daniels inquired icily.

"There's no point in continuing work on the ship," O'Keefe said. "Why waste our time bombing empty bogs?"

"I suggest we keep working on the ship," Tate contradicted.

"Why?" O'Keefe asked.

"So we can head for Fomalhaut and give ourselves up to the hospital station."

Silberman stared at him incredulously. "Turn ourselves in? Why not stay here? We're not harming anybody."

"No, not yet. It's the future I'm thinking of, centuries from now."

"We'll be dead."

"Those of us in this room, sure, but what about our descendants?"

"He's right," Lanoir conceded. "Eventually our descendants will fill this whole solar system. Sooner or later, our ships might spread over the Galaxy." He tried to smile, but his muscles would not respond. "The tapes point out how tenacious paranoids are. They cling fanatically to their fixed beliefs. If our descendants expand into Terran regions, there'll be a fight and we might win because we're more one-track. We would never deviate."

"Fanatics," Daniels whispered.

"We'll have to keep this information from the rest of the camp," O'Keefe said.

"Absolutely," Fisher agreed. "We'll have to keep them thinking the ship is for H-bomb attacks. Otherwise, we'll have one hell of a situation on our hands."

They began moving numbly toward the sealed door.

"Wait a minute," Domgraf-Schwach said urgently. "The two workmen." He started back, while some of them went out into the corridor, the rest back toward their seats.

And then it happened.

Silberman fired first. Fisher screamed as half of him vanished in swirling particles of radioactive ash. Silberman dropped to one knee and fired up at Tate. Tate leaped back and brought out his own B-pistol. Daniels stepped from the path of Lanoir's beam. It missed him and struck the first row of seats.

Lanoir calmly crept along the wall through the billowing clouds of smoke. A figure loomed ahead; he raised his gun and fired. The figure fell to one side and fired back. Lanoir staggered and collapsed like a deflated balloon and Silberman hurried on.

At his desk, Domgraf-Schwach was groping wildly for his escape button. His fingers touched it, but as he depressed the stud, a blast from Portbane's pistol removed the top of his head. The lifeless corpse stood momentarily, then was whisked to "safety" by the intricate apparatus beneath the desk.

"This way!" Portbane shouted, above the sizzle of the B-blasts. "Come on, Tate!"

Various beams were turned in his direction. Half the chamber burst apart and thundered down, disintegrating into rubble and flaming debris. He and Tate scrambled for one of the emergency exits. Behind them, the others hurried, firing savagely.

Horstokowski found the exit and slid past the jammed lock. He fired as the two figures raced up the passage ahead of him. One of them stumbled, but the other grabbed at him and they hobbled off together. Daniels was a better shot. As Tate and Portbane emerged on the surface, one of Daniels' blasts undercut the taller of the two.

Portbane continued running a little way, and then silently pitched face-forward against the side of a plastic house, a gloomy square of opaque blackness against the night sky.

"Where'd they go?" Silberman demanded hoarsely, as he appeared at the mouth of the passage. His right arm had been torn away by Lanoir's blast. The stump was seared hard.

"I got one of them." Daniels and O'Keefe approached the inert figure warily. "It's Portbane. That leaves Tate. We got three of the four. Not bad, on such short notice."

"Tate's damn smart," Silberman panted. "I think he suspected."

He scanned the darkness around them. Soldiers, returning from the gas attack, came hurrying up. Searchlights rumbled toward the scene of the shooting. Off in the distance, sirens wailed.

"Which way did he go?" Daniels asked.

"Over toward the bog."

O'Keefe moved cautiously along the narrow street. The others came slowly behind.

"You were the first to realize," Horstokowski said to Silberman. "For a while, I believed the test. Then I realized we were being tricked—the four of them were plotting in unison."

"I didn't expect four of them," Silberman admitted. "I knew there was at least one Terran spy among us. But Lanoir . . ."

"I always knew Lanoir was a Terran agent," O'Keefe declared flatly. "I wasn't surprised at the test results. They gave themselves away by faking their findings."

Silberman waved over a group of soldiers. "Have Tate picked up and brought here. He's somewhere at the periphery of the camp."

The soldiers hurried away, dazed and muttering. Alarm bells dinned shrilly on all sides. Figures scampered back and forth. Like a disturbed ant colony, the whole camp was alive with excitement.

"In other words," Daniels said, "the four of them really saw the same as we. They saw B as the positive sample, but they put down A instead."

"They knew we'd put down B," O'Keefe said, "since B was the positive sample taken from the attack site. All they had to do was record the opposite. The results seemed to substantiate Lanoir's paranoid theory, which was why Portbane set up the test in the first place. It was planned a long time ago—part of their overall job."

"Lanoir dug up the tapes in the first place!" Daniels exclaimed. "Fisher and he planted them down in the ruins of the ship. Portbane got us to accept his testing device."

"What were they trying to do?" Silberman asked suddenly. "Why were they trying to convince us we're paranoids?"

"Isn't it obvious?" O'Keefe replied. "They wanted us to turn ourselves in. The Terran monkey men naturally are trying to choke off the race that's going to supplant them. We won't surrender, of course. The four of them were clever—they almost had me convinced. When the results flashed up five to four, I had a momentary doubt. But then I realized what an intricate strategy they had worked out."

Horstokowski examined his B-pistol. "I'd like to get hold of Tate and wring the whole story from him, the whole damn account of their planning, so we'd have it in black and white."

"You're still not convinced?" Daniels inquired.

"Of course. But I'd like to hear him admit it."

"I doubt if we'll see Tate again," O'Keefe said. "He must have reached the Terran lines by now. He's probably sitting in a big inter-system military transport, giving his story to gold-braid Terran officials. I'll bet they're moving up heavy guns and shock troops while we stand here."

"We'd better get busy," Daniels said sharply. "We'll repair the ship and load it with H-bombs. After we wipe out their bases here, we'll carry the war to them. A few raids on the Sol System ought to teach them to leave us alone."

Horstokowski grinned. "It'll be an uphill fight—we're alone against a whole galaxy. But I think we'll take care of them. One of us is worth a million Terran monkey men."

Tate lay trembling in the dark tangle of weeds. Dripping black stalks of nocturnal vegetables clutched and stirred around him. Poisonous night insects slithered across the surface of the fetid bog.

He was covered with slime. His clothing was torn and ripped. Somewhere along the way, he had lost his B-pistol. His right shoulder ached; he could hardly move his arm. Bones broken, probably. He was too numb and dazed to care. He lay facedown in the sticky muck and closed his eyes.

He didn't have a chance. Nobody survived in the bogs. He feebly smashed an insect oozing across his neck. It squirmed in his hand and then, reluctantly, died. For a long time, its dead legs kicked.

The probing stalk of a stinging snail began tracing webs across Tate's inert body. As the sticky pressure of the snail crept heavily onto him, he heard the first faint far-off sounds of the camp going into action. For a time, it meant nothing to him. Then he understood—and shuddered miserably, helplessly.

The first phase of the big offensive against Earth was already moving into high gear.

DAW sf BOOKS

Numerical Checklist of DAW BOOKS NEVER BEFORE IN PAPERBACK

UQ1001 SPELL OF THE WITCH WORLD by Andre Norton
UQ1002 THE MIND BEHIND THE EYE by Joseph Green
UQ1003 THE PROBABILITY MAN by Brian N. Ball
UQ1004 THE BOOK OF VAN VOGT
UQ1005 THE 1972 ANNUAL WORLD'S BEST SF
UQ1006 THE DAY STAR by Mark Geston
UQ1007 TO CHALLENGE CHAOS by Brian M. Stableford
UQ1008 THE MINDBLOCKED MAN by Jeff Sutton
UQ1009 TACTICS OF MISTAKE by Gordon R. Dickson
UQ1010 AT THE SEVENTH LEVEL by Suzette Haden Elgin
UQ1011 THE DAY BEFORE TOMORROW by Gerard Klein
UQ1012 A DARKNESS IN MY SOUL by Dean R. Koontz
UQ1013 THE YEAR'S BEST HORROR STORIES
UQ1014 WE CAN BUILD YOU by Philip K. Dick
UQ1015 THE WORLD MENDERS by Lloyd Biggle, Jr.
UQ1016 GENIUS UNLIMITED by John T. Phillifent
UQ1017 BLUE FACE by G. C. Edmondson
UQ1018 CENTURY OF THE MANIKIN by E. C. Tubb
UQ1019 THE REGIMENTS OF NIGHT by Brian N. Ball
UQ1020 OLE DOC METHUSELAH by L. Ron Hubbard
UQ1021 DINOSAUR BEACH by Keith Laumer
UQ1022 THE RETURN OF THE TIME MACHINE by Egon Friedell
UQ1023 THE STARDROPPERS by John Brunner
UQ1024 THE CITY MACHINE by Louis Trimble
UQ1025 MENTION MY NAME IN ATLANTIS by John Jakes
UQ1026 ENTRY TO ELSEWHEN by John Brunner
UQ1027 GREEN PHOENIX by Thomas Burnett Swann
UQ1028 SLEEPWALKER'S WORLD by Gordon R. Dickson
UQ1029 THE BOOK OF BRIAN ALDISS by Brian W. Aldiss
UQ1030 UNDER THE GREEN STAR by Lin Carter
UQ1031 MIRROR IMAGE by Michael G. Coney
UQ1032 THE HALCYON DRIFT by Brian M. Stableford
UQ1033 TRANSIT TO SCORPIO by Alan Burt Akers
UQ1034 THE WANDERING VARIABLES by Louis Trimble
UQ1035 BAPHOMET'S METEOR by Pierre Barbet
UQ1036 DARKOVER LANDFALL by Marion Zimmer Bradley
UQ1037 A TALENT FOR THE INVISIBLE by Ron Goulart
UQ1038 THE LION GAME by James H. Schmitz
UQ1039 THE BOOK OF FRANK HERBERT by Frank Herbert
UQ1040 PLANET PROBABILITY by Brian N. Ball